THRIVE

Cookbook

THRIVE

Cookbook

FOOD THAT FITS YOUR LIFESTYLE

SHELF**RELIANCE**®

TABLE OF CONTENTS

INTRODUCTION

When I was first approached by Shelf Reliance® to develop recipes for THRIVE®, I have to admit, I was a little bit hesitant. As a culinary professional, I am constantly trying to use as much fresh product as possible. Adding freeze-dried and dehydrated products to my repertoire was not exactly something I felt completely comfortable with. Despite my doubts, I took it on as a challenge and looked forward to creating delicious and easy recipes for the THRIVE® family. I wanted to help everyday home cooks find creative ways to incorporate THRIVE® into their daily meals. I appreciated that Shelf Reliance® took their THRIVE® products so seriously and I immediately noticed the amount of time and attention that went into sourcing the best possible products. This made my job easier because I was provided with the best ingredients available.

The approach that Shelf Reliance® takes on THRIVE® is refreshing. Everything from the labels on the cans to the product that is inside is top notch. I kept this approach in mind as I developed recipes for THRIVE®. I spent my days testing recipes that were easy and approachable while still maintaining delicious flavor and incorporating as many THRIVE® ingredients as possible. Along the way, I also enjoyed snacking straight from the cans.

Throughout this book, you will find recipes that I have created, recipes from our consultants, Shelf Reliance® staff, and other culinary professionals that have put their heart and soul into creating outstanding recipes that you can easily make part of your family's everyday life. My best advice is to start small and not overwhelm yourself. Start by adding just one or two THRIVE® ingredients into your daily meals. As you start to use the product line, you will find that cooking with THRIVE® is not nearly as intimidating as you thought it would be. Everything from our freeze-dried berries to our sweet corn can easily be added to recipes with very little effort. It will only be a matter of time before you start coming up with your own signature ways to incorporate THRIVE® ingredients into your favorite dishes!

Kelsey Nixon
Culinary Professional

Meet Kelsey Nixon

Kelsey Nixon got her start in the food media industry when she created *Kelsey's Kitchen*, a college cooking show at Brigham Young University, emphasizing fast, fun, and affordable meals. After graduating with a degree in Broadcast Journalism, she attended Le Cordon Bleu – Hollywood, where she earned her professional culinary arts degree. This degree, paired with training from the French Culinary Institute in New York City, provided opportunities at *Martha Stewart Living* and on the Food Network's *Semi-Homemade Cooking with Sandra Lee*. In 2008, she was a contestant on *The Next Food Network Star*, where she was voted "fan favorite," and went on to star in the Food2 web series "Kelsey and Spike Cook," with Spike Mendelsohn.

Kelsey's passion for the essentials in the kitchen has taken her one step further and she now hosts her own show on the Cooking Channel. In *Kelsey's Essentials*, Kelsey inspires a new generation of food lovers with her own fresh take on essential cooking basics. She gives her savvy tips on must-have pantry items, the latest gadgets and essential kitchen techniques – from roasting to baking. Kelsey's passion is creating recipes that target the beginning cook – breaking down the basics, teaching proper technique and making everyone feel comfortable in the kitchen.

Kelsey lives in New York City with her husband Robby where she spends her days developing recipes and cooking up a storm.

THRIVE

YOUR FAVORITE FOODS...REDEFINED

THRIVE® lets you experience your favorite foods in a new way. People love THRIVE® because it is easy to cook with and they enjoy the convenience of having so many healthy choices right at their fingertips. Come experience THRIVE®, and enjoy your favorite foods, redefined.

CONVENIENT

The THRIVE® food line consists of the same foods you would purchase at the market, only with THRIVE® you don't have to dash to the store every time you run out of essential ingredients. Most THRIVE® products can be used right out of the can, so your meals will be ready to eat in no time at all.

LONG-LASTING

Most THRIVE® products have an optimal sealed shelf life of 10-20 years and an opened shelf life of 6-18 months. Many THRIVE® foods undergo a natural preservation process called freeze drying. This innovative process locks in the taste and freshness of each THRIVE® food, allowing you to enjoy the same great taste for years to come.

AFFORDABLE

Incorporating THRIVE® into your daily diet can literally save you hundreds of dollars each year. By reallocating a portion of your monthly food budget to THRIVE® foods, you will start to build your THRIVE® Home Store with healthy, great tasting foods in no time at all.

HEALTHY & DELICIOUS

THRIVE® products are all-natural, so naturally they are good for you. Each product is organized into one of six recognized and trusted categories to make it easy for you to maintain a well-balanced diet. THRIVE® foods are developed with proper nutrition in mind, so you can feel confident that when you eat THRIVE®, you are guiding your family to a healthy and happy life.

FREEZE DRYING PROCESS

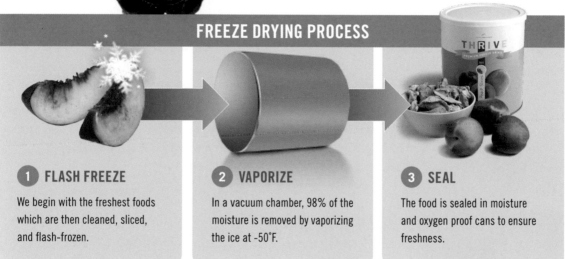

1 FLASH FREEZE

We begin with the freshest foods which are then cleaned, sliced, and flash-frozen.

2 VAPORIZE

In a vacuum chamber, 98% of the moisture is removed by vaporizing the ice at -50°F.

3 SEAL

The food is sealed in moisture and oxygen proof cans to ensure freshness.

4 ENJOY!

When the water is replaced, THRIVE® foods regain their original fresh flavor, aroma, nutrients, texture, and appearance, making them perfect for everyday cooking and snacking.

THRIVE® TIPS

HALF WHITE/HALF WHEAT

To add an extra boost of nutrition to your white breads, add half whole wheat flour to your recipes. This will add a delicious flavor and it is a great way to utilize your whole wheat. The half white/half wheat ratio can be used in almost any situation whether you are making breads, desserts, or thickening a stew. Keep in mind that whole wheat flour is heavier and may need more leavening such as slightly increasing the yeast in a recipe or increasing the baking powder by ½ teaspoon for every 1½ cups of whole wheat flour used.

BABY FOOD

Your THRIVE® freeze-dried fruits and vegetables can be used to make delicious homemade baby food that is free from harmful preservatives. Simply rehydrate the product as directed on the can, adding any desired flavors, and purée in a blender or food processor. Freeze puréed fruits and vegetables in ice cube trays for serving sizes and store in freezer bags until ready to use.

ADDING A FRESH TOUCH

As you develop a system to integrate THRIVE® products into your daily meals, try mixing it with fresh ingredients. This is a great way to experiment with THRIVE® in recipes that your family already loves. THRIVE® powdered milk and eggs are a great place to start. Our freeze-dried berries are another group of ingredients that you can easily toss into cereal or bake into desserts. With so many great tasting and easy-to-use ingredients, the possibilities are endless.

BUTTER POWDER

THRIVE® Butter Powder is best used as a spreadable butter for topping toast, fresh breads, or even making your own honey butter. You can also utilize this product anytime you want to add butter flavor to a dish like a casserole, sauce, or gravy. If you choose to use your butter powder in baking, mix the powder with the dry ingredients before baking. Results vary with baking.

To rehydrate THRIVE® Butter Powder combine ½ cup powder + ¼ cup water.

THRIVE® EQUIVALENTS

To rehydrate THRIVE® freeze-dried or dehydrated foods, place the product in a dish or bowl and cover with warm water for 10-15 minutes. Once the food has completely rehydrated, drain off any remaining liquid. For faster rehydration, use hot or boiling water. Do not use this method for THRIVE® Fruit.

INGREDIENT	THRIVE®	FRESH	INGREDIENT	THRIVE®	FRESH
Fruit *(Some fruit equivalents are based on weight, not quantity)*			Broccoli (FD)	1 cup + 1 cup water	1 cup broccoli
Apple Chips	1 cup + 1 cup water	1 medium apple	Carrot Dices	1 cup + 1 cup water	2 cups carrots, diced
Apples Slices	1 cup + 1 cup water	1 medium apple	Cauliflower (FD)	1 cup + ½ cup water	1 cup cauliflower
Apricots (FD)	1 cup + 1 cup water	1 apricot	Celery (FD)	1 cup + ½ cup water	1 cup celery, diced
Banana Slices (FD)	1 cup + 1 cup water	1 banana	Green Beans (FD)	1 cup + ½ cup water	1 cup green beans
Blackberries (FD)	1 cup + 1 cup water	1 cup blackberries	Green Peas (FD)	1 cup + ½ cup water	1 cup green peas
Blueberries (FD)	1 cup + 1 cup water	1 cup blueberries	Mushroom Pieces (FD)	1 cup + ½ cup water	1 cup mushrooms, chopped
Mandarin Oranges (FD)	1 cup + 1 cup water	8 oz. can oranges	Onions	⅓ cup + ⅓ cup water	1 small white onion
Mangoes (FD)	1 cup + 1 cup water	1 mango, sliced	Onions (FD)	1 cup + 1 cup water	1 small white onion
Peaches (FD)	1 cup + 1 cup water	1 peach, sliced	Potato Beads	2 cups + ⅔ cup milk + 3 T butter + 2 cups water	3 ¼ cups mashed potatoes
Pears (FD)	1 cup + 1 cup water	1 pear, sliced	Potato Chunks	⅔ cup + 1 cup water	1 medium potato, boiled
Pineapple Chunks (FD)	1 cup + 1 cup water	1 cup pineapple	Potato Dices (FD)	1 cup + 1 cup water	1 cup potatoes, diced
Raspberries (FD)	1 cup + 1 cup water	1 cup raspberries	Spinach (FD)	1 cup + ¾ cup water	1 cup spinach, cooked
Meats *(Weight based on drained product)*			Sweet Corn (FD)	1 cup + 1 cup water	1 cup corn
Chicken (FD)	2½ cups + 2 cups water	1 lb. chicken	Sweet Potato	⅔ cup + 1 cup water	1 medium potato, boiled
Ground Beef (FD)	2½ cups + 2 cups water	1 lb. ground beef	Tomato Powder	¼ cup + ½ cup water	6 oz. or ¾ cup tomato paste
Ham (FD)	2½ cups + 2 cups water	1 lb. ham	**Dairy**		
Roast Beef (FD)	2⅓ cups + 2 cups water	1 lb. roast beef	Instant Milk	6 T + 1 cup water	1 cup milk
Sausage (FD)	2½ cups + 2 cups water	1 lb. sausage	Powdered Milk	3 T + 1 cup water	1 cup milk
Turkey (FD)	2½ cups + 2 cups water	1 lb. turkey	**Basics** *(Consistency can be altered to suit individual preference)*		
TVP			Butter Powder	½ cup + ¼ cup water	1 stick of butter (½ cup)
Bacon TVP	1½ cups + 1 cup water	1 lb. bacon	Shortening	1 cup + ¼ cup water	1 cup shortening
Beef TVP	1½ cups + 1½ cups water	1 lb. ground beef	Sour Cream	1 cup + 1 cup water	1 cup sour cream
Chicken TVP	2 cups + 2 cups water	1 lb. chicken			
Ham TVP	1⅓ cups + 1⅓ cups water	1 lb. ham			
Sausage TVP	2½ cups + 2½ cups water	1 lb. sausage			
Sloppy Joe TVP	2 cups + 2 cups water	1 lb. ground beef + seasoning			
Taco TVP	1¼ cups + 1¼ cups water	1 lb. ground beef + seasoning			
Vegetables					
Bell Peppers	½ cup + 1 cup water	1 bell pepper			

MILK MIXTURES

INSTANT MILK vs. POWDERED MILK

THRIVE® Instant Milk is a great alternative to regular milk when thoroughly mixed and kept very cold. You could even add vanilla or sugar for an extra boost of flavor. THRIVE® Powdered Milk is better for baking and cooking purposes. Any recipe that calls for milk can be replaced with powdered milk. Simply add the correct amount of powdered milk to the dry ingredients and then add water for the milk called for in the recipe.

THRIVE® INSTANT MILK			
THRIVE® INSTANT MILK	+ WATER	=	YIELD
1½ tablespoons	¼ cup		¼ cup milk
2 tablespoons	⅓ cup		⅓ cup milk
3 tablespoons	½ cup		½ cup milk
4 tablespoons	⅔ cup		⅔ cup milk
4½ tablespoons	¾ cup		¾ cup milk
6 tablespoons	1 cup		1 cup milk

THRIVE® POWDERED MILK			
THRIVE® POWDERED MILK	+ WATER	=	YIELD
¾ tablespoon	¼ cup		¼ cup milk
1 tablespoon	⅓ cup		⅓ cup milk
1½ tablespoons	½ cup		½ cup milk
2 tablespoons	⅔ cup		⅔ cup milk
2¼ tablespoons	¾ cup		¾ cup milk
3 tablespoons	1 cup		1 cup milk

The milk ratios shown above are based on a consistency suited to the recipes included in this cookbook. Milk consistency may be altered to suit individual preference.

SWEETENED CONDENSED MILK							
THRIVE® POWDERED MILK	+	HOT WATER	+	BUTTER (SOFTENED)	+	SUGAR	+	VANILLA	=	SWEETENED CONDENSED MILK
1 cup		½ cup		2 tablespoons		1 cup		½ teaspoon		14 oz.

Pour milk powder, hot water, and butter into a blender or food processor. Gradually add sugar and vanilla, beating well until fully incorporated. Store in refrigerator. Mixture will thicken slightly as it stands.

BUTTERMILK				
THRIVE® POWDERED MILK	+	VINEGAR OR LEMON JUICE	+ WATER	=	BUTTERMILK
3 tablespoons		3 tablespoons	1 cup		1 cup

Mix and let stand 3 to 5 minutes.

EVAPORATED MILK			
THRIVE® POWDERED MILK	+	WATER	=	EVAPORATED MILK
9 tablespoons		1½ cups		12 oz

Blend until thoroughly mixed (replaces half and half).

BEAN BASICS

Sort the beans removing any debris, empty shells or discolored beans.
Then put the beans in a colander or strainer and rinse.

QUICK SOAK

Add 4 cups of water for every 1 cup of beans that you wish to soak. Bring
the water to a rapid boil and then remove from heat and let stand for 1 hour
before using. Don't boil the beans for too long or you may damage the skins.

OVERNIGHT SOAK

Add 4 cups of water for every 1 cup of beans that you wish to soak. Soak
beans overnight. Overnight soaking of beans will make them more digestible
so less intestinal gas is usually produced after you eat them.

BEAN VARIETY (SOAKED)	COOK TIME
Black	1 to 1½ hours
Kidney	1 to 1½ hours
Lentils (no soaking)	30 – 45 minutes
Lima	45 – 60 minutes
Pinto	1 to 1½ hours
Small Red	1 to 1½ hours
Small White Navy	1 to 1½ hours

USING BEANS AS A FAT REPLACEMENT

For a healthier option for baked goods, try replacing oil, butter, or margarine with THRIVE® beans. After following our proper bean cooking guidelines,
simply mash the beans in a blender or a food processor until the beans are the consistency of shortening. Adjust the consistency by adding water if
necessary. You can replace the beans for fat using a 1 to 1 ratio. For example, if a recipe calls for ½ cup butter, use ½ cup mashed beans. Remember
to use the type of bean that best matches what you are baking so that the product will still look the same. For chocolate based desserts use black
beans and for sugar cookies use white beans.

EASY EGGS

THRIVE® Whole Eggs are a quick and easy solution to all your baking needs, and because these eggs come in a powder they are guaranteed to be safe. Each
can of THRIVE® Whole Eggs has a 5 year sealed shelf life and our #10 can contains well over 100 servings, so you won't need to worry about running out of this
essential ingredient for a very long time.

EGGS	THRIVE® WHOLE EGGS	WATER
1 egg	1 tablespoon	2 tablespoons
2 eggs	2 tablespoons	¼ cup
3 eggs	3 tablespoons	6 tablespoons

Peach Smoothie, page 27

APPETIZERS, SNACKS & BEVERAGES

If you really want to make a friend, go to someone's house and eat with him...the people who give you their food give you their heart.

Cesar Chavez

THRIVE® FOODS

- Sweet Corn
- Black Beans
- Pinto Beans
- White Sugar
- Iodized Salt

- May be exchanged for fresh ingredients.

BLACK BEAN & CORN SALSA

This salsa is a perfect way to utilize your dried beans and the sweet corn really takes the recipe from good to great. Try it with our quick and easy quesadillas.

SERVES 10 • PREP TIME: 10 min • TOTAL TIME: 10 min

1¼ cups THRIVE® Black Beans, rinsed and cooked
1¼ cups THRIVE® Pinto Beans, rinsed and cooked
¾ cup THRIVE® Sweet Corn *(FD)*
1 (4 oz) can chopped green chiles, undrained
½ small red onion, finely chopped
¼ cup cilantro leaves, finely chopped
¼ cup red wine vinegar
½ cup vegetable oil
¼ cup THRIVE® White Sugar
    THRIVE® Iodized Salt and cracked black pepper to taste

1 Cook beans if needed. Directions can be found on page 13.

2 In a small bowl, add corn and cover with warm water. Let sit 5-10 minutes or until corn is softened and rehydrated. Drain.

3 Mix the black beans, pinto beans, corn, green chiles, red onion, and cilantro together in a large bowl.

4 To make the dressing, stir the vinegar, vegetable oil, and sugar together in a pan. Bring to a boil, then remove from heat, and cool. Pour dressing over bean mixture, and toss to mix evenly.

Appetizers, Snacks & Beverages

QUICK & EASY QUESADILLAS

Nothing beats homemade Mexican food!

SERVES 6 • PREP TIME: 15 min • TOTAL TIME: 20 min

 1 cup THRIVE® Taco TVP
 ¼ cup THRIVE® Mixed Bell Peppers
 1 tablespoon THRIVE® Chopped Onions *(FD)*
1½ cups boiling water
 1 teaspoon vegetable oil
 6 six-inch flour tortillas
4½ cups THRIVE® Shredded Cheddar Cheese
 ½ cup THRIVE® Sour Cream, *optional*
     (½ cup powder + ½ cup water)
     salsa, *optional*

1 Place TVP, red and green peppers, and onion in a large bowl and cover with warm water. Allow the TVP and vegetables to sit for 5-10 minutes or until water is absorbed and the ingredients are rehydrated. Drain. Repeat process in a different bowl for the Cheddar cheese making sure all of the water has been drained from the cheese.

2 Heat vegetable oil in a medium-sized pan over medium-low heat. Place a tortilla in the pan and sprinkle with ½ cup rehydrated cheese. Add ½ cup of drained Taco TVP and vegetable mixture over the cheese, followed by another ½ cup of rehydrated cheese.

3 Cover cheese, TVP, and vegetables with another tortilla. Cook for 2-3 minutes or until golden brown. Flip and cook for an additional 2 minutes. Remove quesadilla from pan and cut into wedges. Repeat process with remaining ingredients. Serve with sour cream and salsa, if desired.

Tip *from the* Kitchen

Try using our Whole Wheat Flour Tortilla recipe found on page 53.

Try this recipe with our Black Bean & Corn salsa found on page 17.

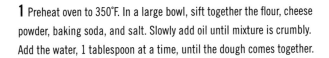

CHEDDAR CHEESE CRISPS

This recipe is fun to make with kids!
It's a healthy snack they are sure to love.

SERVES 8 • PREP TIME: 10 min **• TOTAL TIME:** 25 min

1¼ cups THRIVE® Whole Wheat or White Flour
½ cup THRIVE® Cheese Blend
⅛ teaspoon THRIVE® Baking Soda
¼ teaspoon THRIVE® Iodized Salt
3 tablespoons vegetable oil
½ cup water

1 Preheat oven to 350°F. In a large bowl, sift together the flour, cheese powder, baking soda, and salt. Slowly add oil until mixture is crumbly. Add the water, 1 tablespoon at a time, until the dough comes together.

2 Roll out dough on a well floured surface; about ⅛ inch thick. Transfer to a greased baking sheet. Divide dough into small squares with a large knife or pizza cutter. Prick the tops of each square and sprinkle with salt.

3 Bake for 10-15 minutes or until golden brown. Cool before removing crackers from sheet pan.

Tip *from the* Kitchen

You can also use THRIVE® Mac & Cheese Powder in place of Cheese Blend.

WHOLE WHEAT CRACKERS

Make a variety of different flavors just by adding a few basic ingredients.

SERVES 16 • PREP TIME: 30 min • TOTAL TIME: 1 hour

1½ cups THRIVE® White Flour
½ cup THRIVE® Whole Wheat Flour
½ cup THRIVE® White Sugar
¼ teaspoon THRIVE® Iodized Salt
2 tablespoons butter, softened
⅔ cup THRIVE® Powdered Milk, rehydrated
  (2 tablespoons powder + ⅔ cup water)
  additional ingredients for variations, see tip

1 Preheat oven to 350°F. Combine flours, sugar, and salt. Cut in butter and mix until crumbly.

2 Slowly add milk until dough comes together.

3 Roll out on floured surface about ⅛ inch thick and cut into squares or desired shapes. Prick with fork.

4 Bake for 30-35 minutes or until crisp and light brown.

Tip *from the* Kitchen

To add variety to your whole wheat crackers, divide the dough into quarters and add any of the following ingredients:

To each quarter, add:
- ¼ cup THRIVE® Bacon TVP, rehydrated
- 2 tablespoons Parmesan cheese + ¼ teaspoon salt
- 1 teaspoon dried Rosemary + 1 teaspoon granulated garlic
- sprinkle prepared dough generously with onion salt

To make a full recipe of one of the variations listed above, simply quadruple the suggested amount and add to the full recipe.

Appetizers, Snacks & Beverages

CINNAMON SUGAR GRAHAM CRACKERS

This is a fantastic recipe to make with children. By incorporating whole wheat flour it provides a boost of nutrition and great flavor.

SERVES 24 • PREP TIME: 15 min • TOTAL TIME: 1 hour 15 min

2 cups THRIVE® Whole Wheat Flour
1 cup THRIVE® White Flour
1 teaspoon THRIVE® Baking Powder
½ teaspoon THRIVE® Baking Soda
½ cup butter, softened
½ cup THRIVE® Brown Sugar, packed
⅓ cup honey
½ cup THRIVE® Powdered Milk, rehydrated
 (1½ tablespoons powder+ ½ cup water)
2 teaspoons vanilla extract
1 tablespoon cinnamon
2 tablespoons THRIVE® White Sugar

1 Sift together the whole wheat flour, white flour, baking powder and baking soda; set aside.

2 In a medium-sized bowl, cream together the butter, brown sugar, and honey until light and fluffy. Stir in the sifted ingredients alternating between the milk and vanilla. Cover dough and chill in refrigerator for at least an hour.

3 Preheat the oven to 350°F. Divide the chilled dough into quarters.

4 On a well-floured surface, roll the dough out one quarter at a time into a large rectangle (dough should be ⅛ inch thick). Divide into smaller rectangles using a knife. Place rectangles on ungreased baking sheets. Mark a line down the center of each one without cutting through the dough, and prick the tops with a fork.

5 Combine cinnamon and white sugar and sprinkle over dough before baking. Bake for 8 to 10 minutes in the preheated oven or until edges are golden brown. Remove from baking sheets to cool on wire racks.

Appetizers, Snacks & Beverages

COCONUT ALMOND FRUIT GRANOLA

This granola will add a deliciously fruity crunch to any breakfast.

SERVES 6 • PREP TIME: 10 min • TOTAL TIME: 30 min

2 cups THRIVE® Quick Oats
¾ cup almonds, slivered
½ cup sweetened flaked coconut
½ cup cashews
⅓ cup THRIVE® Brown Sugar
½ teaspoon ground allspice
1½ teaspoons ground cinnamon
¼ cup unsalted butter
2 tablespoons honey
¼ cup THRIVE® Pears *(FD)*
¼ cup THRIVE® Raspberries *(FD)*
¼ cup THRIVE® Blueberries *(FD)*

1 Preheat oven to 300°F.

2 Mix first 7 ingredients in large bowl (quick oats through cinnamon).

3 Melt butter with honey in a small, heavy saucepan over low heat. Pour over granola mixture and toss well. Spread mixture on baking sheet.

4 Bake 20-25 minutes, stirring occasionally. Continue to bake until granola is golden brown, stirring frequently, about 5 minutes longer. Cool. Toss with freeze-dried fruits. Store in an airtight container at room temperature.

Tip *from the* Kitchen

Serve this granola over yogurt, oatmeal, or even ice cream.

CHEWY GRANOLA BARS

The perfect healthy snack that you can pack for a hike or outdoor picnic.

SERVES 12 • PREP TIME: 15 min • TOTAL TIME: 1 hour

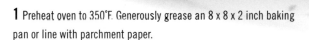

1⅔ cups THRIVE® Quick Oats
¾ cup THRIVE® White Sugar
⅓ cup THRIVE® Whole Wheat Flour
½ teaspoon THRIVE® Iodized Salt
½ teaspoon ground cinnamon
2½ cups THRIVE® freeze-dried fruit
6 tablespoons butter, melted
¼ cup honey
2 tablespoons light corn syrup
1 tablespoon water
⅓ cup peanut butter

1 Preheat oven to 350°F. Generously grease an 8 x 8 x 2 inch baking pan or line with parchment paper.

2 In a small bowl, add freeze-dried fruit and rehydrate by covering with warm water for 5-10 minutes until fruit is softened and rehydrated. Drain.

3 In a large bowl, mix together the dry ingredients. Stir in the rehydrated fruit that has been thoroughly drained in addition to any other ingredients you would like to add (nuts, coconut, chocolate chips, raisins, etc.) In a separate bowl, whisk together the melted butter, honey, corn syrup, and water. Mix the wet ingredients into the dry ingredients including the peanut butter until the mixture is fully incorporated (mixture will be moist).

4 Spread in the prepared pan and press down to make sure the mixture covers the entire pan. Bake the bars for 25-35 minutes or until the edges are golden brown. Cool the bars in the pan completely. Once cool, remove from pan and use a knife to cut the bars into the desired shape. Removing the bars before completely cooling can result in a crumbly bar. If necessary, finish cooling the bars in the pan in the refrigerator to speed up the process and allow them to fully set. Store bars in an airtight container. Bars can be frozen.

Tip *from the* Kitchen

Get creative with this recipe! Add your favorite THRIVE® fruits in addition to nuts, coconut, chocolate chips, or raisins.

STRAWBERRY BANANA FREEZE

SERVES 2 • PREP TIME: 10 min • TOTAL TIME: 10 min

½ cup THRIVE® Orange Drink, rehydrated
   (1 tablespoon powder + ½ cup water)
1½ cups cold water
½ cup THRIVE® Pineapple Chunks *(FD)*
1 cup THRIVE® Strawberries *(FD)*
1 cup THRIVE® Banana Slices *(FD)*
1 cup ice cubes

1 Combine the orange drink, water, pineapple, strawberries, bananas, and ice in a blender and process until smooth. Refrigerate until cold.

PEACH SMOOTHIE

SERVES 2 • PREP TIME: 10 min • TOTAL TIME: 10 min

1 cup THRIVE® Peach Slices *(FD)*
1 cup vanilla yogurt
1 cup ice cubes
2 tablespoons THRIVE® White Sugar

1 Combine all ingredients in a blender and blend until smooth. Add more ice cubes or vanilla yogurt to reach desired consistency. Serve immediately.

VERY ORANGE BERRY SMOOTHIE

SERVES 2 • PREP TIME: 10 min • TOTAL TIME: 10 min

1 cup THRIVE® Orange Drink, rehydrated
   (2 tablespoons powder + 1 cup water)
1 cup THRIVE® freeze-dried berries *(any variety)*
1 cup ice cream or frozen yogurt
⅓ cup ice cubes

1 In a small bowl, add freeze-dried berries and cover with THRIVE® Orange Drink until soft and rehydrated.

2 Partially drain berries and blend with other ingredients. Garnish with additional berries, fruit, and whipped cream, if desired.

BERRY SMOOTHIE

SERVES 2 • PREP TIME: 10 min • TOTAL TIME: 10 min

2 tablespoons THRIVE® Peach Drink, dry
1 cup water
½ cup THRIVE® Peach Slices *(FD)**
½ cup THRIVE® Blackberries *(FD)**
1½ cups ice cubes
¼ cup THRIVE® Instant Milk, dry

1 In a blender mix 2 tablespoons peach drink powder with one cup of water. Add peach slices and blackberries to the drink mix. Add ice and instant milk powder then blend until smooth.

*Substitute with any THRIVE® freeze-dried fruit variety.

BREADS & GRAINS

If thou tastest a crust of bread, thou tastest all the stars and all the heavens.

Robert Browning

30 Minute Rolls, page 45

BLACKBERRY MUFFIN CUPS
These simple muffins are bursting with flavor.

SERVES 12 • PREP TIME: 15 min • TOTAL TIME: 40 min

¾ cup light ricotta cheese
1 cup THRIVE® Blackberries *(FD)*
2 THRIVE® Whole Eggs, rehydrated
(2 tablespoons powder + 4 tablespoons water)
1 teaspoon vanilla
½ cup butter, softened
½ cup THRIVE® White Sugar
    zest of 1 orange, finely grated
1 cup THRIVE® White Flour
1 cup THRIVE® Whole Wheat Flour
2 teaspoons THRIVE® Baking Powder
¼ teaspoon THRIVE® Baking Soda
½ teaspoon THRIVE® Iodized Salt
¾ cup water

1 Preheat oven to 400°F and line muffin tin with muffin cups. In a small bowl, cover blackberries with warm water. Let sit 5-10 minutes until softened and rehydrated. Drain.

2 In a separate mixing bowl, whisk together the ricotta, eggs, and vanilla, then mix in the butter.

3 In another large bowl, whisk sugar and orange zest together until the sugar is moist and fragrant. Stir in the flour, baking powder, baking soda, and salt.

4 Incorporate ricotta mixture into the dry ingredients. Use a rubber spatula to gently and quickly blend the mixtures together, while slowly adding ¾ cup water to mixture.

5 Gently fold in the drained, rehydrated blackberries. Divide batter evenly among the muffin cups. Bake for 20-25 minutes or until muffin tops are golden brown.

Breads & Grains

30

SWEET POTATO MUFFINS

A unique muffin that is delightfully moist and tasty.

SERVES 24 • PREP TIME: 30 min • TOTAL TIME: 45 min

1 cup THRIVE® Sweet Potatoes

½ cup apple juice *or THRIVE® Apple Drink*

½ cup THRIVE® Powdered Milk, rehydrated
   (1½ tablespoons powder + ½ cup hot water)

¼ cup vegetable oil

2 THRIVE® Whole Eggs, rehydrated
   (2 tablespoons powder + 4 tablespoons water)

½ cup honey

1½ cups THRIVE® White Flour

1 tablespoon THRIVE® Baking Powder

½ teaspoon THRIVE® Baking Soda

½ teaspoon THRIVE® Iodized Salt

2 teaspoons cinnamon

1 cup butterscotch chips

1 Preheat oven to 350°F. Boil 3 cups water and cook 1 cup sweet potatoes for 15-20 minutes until soft and rehydrated, or until the water is nearly gone. No need to drain.

2 Purée sweet potatoes, apple juice, prepared milk, oil, prepared eggs, and honey in food processor or blender.

3 In a large mixing bowl combine dry ingredients (flour through cinnamon). Add the sweet potato mixture to dry ingredients. Mix only until combined. Batter will be thick and sticky. Add butterscotch chips to slightly cooled batter.

4 Spoon batter into muffin cups, filling about ⅔ full. Bake 23-25 minutes. (For mini muffins bake about 10-12 minutes.) Best if not over cooked to keep them soft and moist.

BLUEBERRY MUFFINS WITH STREUSEL TOPPING

These muffins will bring even more joy to the breakfast table because the crunchy streusel topping is sure to leave your family smiling.

SERVES 18 • PREP TIME: 25 min • TOTAL TIME: 45 min

3 cups THRIVE® Blueberries *(FD)*

¾ cup butter, softened and divided

1¾ cups THRIVE® White Sugar

2 THRIVE® Whole Eggs, rehydrated
(2 tablespoons powder + 2 tablespoons water)

2⅓ cups THRIVE® White Flour

2 teaspoons THRIVE® Baking Powder

½ teaspoon THRIVE® Iodized Salt

½ cup THRIVE® Powdered Milk, rehydrated
(3 tablespoons powder + ½ cup water)

½ teaspoon ground cinnamon

1 Preheat oven to 375°F.
In a medium-sized bowl, cover freeze-dried blueberries with hot water. Let sit 5-10 minutes or until softened and rehydrated. Drain.

2 In a large mixing bowl, cream ½ cup softened butter and 1¼ cups white sugar. Whisk in prepared eggs.

3 In another bowl, combine dry ingredients; 2 cups flour, baking powder, and salt. Incorporate dry ingredients into creamed mixture alternately with the prepared milk. Fold in drained blueberries.

4 Fill greased or paper-lined muffin cups ⅔ full.

5 In a small bowl, combine cinnamon with remaining sugar (½ cup) and flour (⅓ cup) and cut in remaining butter (¼ cup) until crumbly. Sprinkle over muffins.

6 Bake muffins for 15-20 minutes or until an inserted toothpick comes out clean. Cool for 5 minutes before removing from pan to wire racks. Serve muffins warm.

BERRY CINNAMON ROLLS
WITH LEMON CREAM CHEESE ICING

I didn't think it was possible to make cinnamon rolls any more delicious!

SERVES 24 • PREP TIME: 30 min • TOTAL TIME: 1 hour 30 min

Cinnamon Rolls:

- 2¼ teaspoons active dry yeast
- ½ cup warm water
- 6½ cups THRIVE® White Flour or Whole Wheat Flour
- ¾ cup THRIVE® White Sugar
- 1 teaspoon THRIVE® Iodized Salt
- 2 THRIVE® Whole Eggs, rehydrated
  (2 tablespoons powder + ¼ cup water)
- 2 cups THRIVE® Powdered Milk, rehydrated
  (6 tablespoons powder + 2 cups water)
- 2 tablespoons butter, softened
- ½ cup THRIVE® Brown Sugar
- 1 tablespoon cinnamon
- ½ cup butter, melted
- 2 cups THRIVE® freeze-dried berries *(any variety)*

Icing:

- ¼ cup butter, softened
- ¼ cup cream cheese, softened
- 2-3 teaspoons THRIVE® Powdered Milk *(prepared)*
- 1 teaspoon vanilla
  zest of 1 lemon
- 2 cups THRIVE® Powdered Sugar

1 Combine water, yeast, and a pinch of sugar in a small bowl. Let sit for 5 minutes until bubbly.

2 In another bowl, mix prepared eggs and prepared milk. Next, add water/yeast mixture from step 1.

3 In another large bowl, mix together dry ingredients; flour, sugar, and salt. Next, combine wet and dry ingredients to form a dough. Scrape down sides as needed. Mix in 2 tablespoons softened butter just until incorporated. Knead for 5 minutes either using a dough hook on a stand mixer or by hand. Cover and let rise until doubled in size.

4 In a small bowl, cover freeze-dried fruit with warm water and let sit for 5 -10 minutes until berries are softened and rehydrated. Drain.

5 After dough has risen, punch down. Roll dough out to 24 x 12 inches. Spread with ½ cup melted butter and sprinkle with brown sugar and cinnamon. Top with rehydrated berries.

6 Preheat oven to 350°F. Starting with the long side, roll up dough tightly ending with the seam side down. Cut approximately 24 slices each about 1 inch thick. Place slices on a greased cookie sheet. Cover and let rise again for an additional 20-30 minutes, then bake for 17-20 minutes or until rolls are golden brown.

For Lemon Cream Cheese Icing:

1 In a medium-sized mixing bowl, blend softened butter and cream cheese together, then add 2-3 teaspoons milk, vanilla, and lemon zest.

2 Whip in powdered sugar, adding more for a thicker icing and less for thinner consistency. More milk may be added if icing becomes too thick.

CINNAMON SUGAR SCONES

These scones come together quickly and the cinnamon sugar flavor really seals the deal.

SERVES 8 • PREP TIME: 15 min • TOTAL TIME: 30 min

Scones:
- 2 cups THRIVE® White Flour
- 3 teaspoons THRIVE® Baking Powder
- ½ teaspoon THRIVE® Iodized Salt
- 3 tablespoons THRIVE® White Sugar
- 3 teaspoons cinnamon
- 1¼ cups heavy cream

Icing:
- 1 cup THRIVE® Powdered Sugar
- 1 teaspoon vanilla
- 1 teaspoon cinnamon
- 2-3 tablespoons THRIVE® Powdered Milk, rehydrated
   (1½ teaspoons powder + 3 tablespoons water)

1 Preheat oven to 400°F.

2 In a large mixing bowl, mix together flour, baking powder, salt, sugar, and cinnamon. Slowly add heavy cream. Mix or knead by hand, just until combined (about 1 minute). Mix will be sticky.

3 On a well-floured surface divide dough into two sections and form into two rounds, each approximately four inches in diameter and ¼ inch thick.

4 Score each round first with a knife into 4ths, then 8ths. Then cut and place on a greased baking sheet. Bake for 12 to 14 minutes or until edges are golden brown. Cool for 5 minutes before icing.

For Icing:

1 In a medium-sized mixing bowl, mix ingredients together until you achieve a thin icing consistency and drizzle over warm scones. If icing is too thick, thin with additional milk.

6 GRAIN PANCAKES WITH BERRY COMPOTE

Thrive® 6 Grain Pancake mix is delicious on its own, but by adding this simple berry compote your pancakes will go from pleasing to perfect!

SERVES 8 • PREP TIME: 15 min • TOTAL TIME: 30 min

Pancakes:

- 3 cups THRIVE® 6 Grain Pancake Mix
- 2 cups THRIVE® Powdered Milk, rehydrated
  (6 tablespoons powder + 2 cups water)
- 2 THRIVE® Whole Eggs, rehydrated
  (2 tablespoons powder + ¼ cup water)
- ¾ cup THRIVE® freeze-dried berries *(any variety)*

Berry Compote:

- 2 cups THRIVE® freeze-dried berries *(any variety)*
- 1 cup THRIVE® Peach Drink or Apple Drink, rehydrated
  (2 tablespoons drink mix + 1 cup water)
- ⅓ cup THRIVE® White Sugar

1 Blend pancake mix with milk and eggs in a medium-sized mixing bowl. Gently stir together; add berries to taste.

2 Cook in a frying pan or on a griddle, using butter or non-stick spray to keep the pancakes from sticking and falling apart. Flip once and cook through. Serve with warm berry compote and cream.

For berry compote:

1 Place 2 cups berries into a small saucepan. Cover with prepared apple or peach drink; add sugar.

2 Simmer over medium-high heat to boiling, stirring occasionally. Continue boiling and stirring until berries reach syrupy consistency. Serve over pancakes or alongside ice cream, waffles, or other desserts.

Tip *from the* Kitchen

Try these with our whipped cream recipe on page 127.

BANANA PANCAKES WITH SWEET CREAM CINNAMON SPREAD

You will wake up early, even on a Saturday, just to eat these wonderful pancakes.

SERVES 6 • PREP TIME: 15 min • TOTAL TIME: 30 min

Pancakes:
- ¾ cup THRIVE® Banana Slices *(FD)*
- 1½ cups THRIVE® Powdered Milk, rehydrated
  (6 tablespoons powder + 1½ cups water)
- 2 THRIVE® Whole Eggs, rehydrated
  (2 tablespoons powder + ¼ cup water)
- ¼ cup THRIVE® White Sugar
- 1 teaspoon vanilla
- 1½ cups THRIVE® Whole Wheat Flour
- 3 teaspoons THRIVE® Baking Powder
- ¾ teaspoon cinnamon
- ¾ teaspoon THRIVE® Iodized Salt

Sweet Cream Cinnamon Spread:
- ½ cup cream cheese, softened
- ½ cup whipped cream
  THRIVE® Powdered Milk as needed *(prepared)*
- 1 teaspoon cinnamon
- ¼ cup THRIVE® White Sugar
- ½ teaspoon vanilla

1 In a medium-sized bowl, cover bananas in warm water for 5-10 minutes or until soft and rehydrated. Drain.

2 Mash banana slices in a large bowl. Add the prepared milk, prepared eggs, sugar, and vanilla.

3 Combine whole wheat flour in a small bowl with baking powder, cinnamon, and salt.

4 Sift dry mixture into wet ingredients and stir until combined. Make into pancakes using a hot griddle. You could also use this recipe for waffles, adding flour as needed.

For Sweet Cream Cinnamon Spread:

1 Add cream cheese to whipped cream. If mixture becomes too thick, add milk by the tablespoon until you reach a consistency that can be drizzled over the pancakes.

2 Add in cinnamon and sugar; serve with pancakes or waffles.

APPLE PUFF PANCAKES

These pancakes give a fun and fruity twist to a classic breakfast dish.

SERVES 4-6 • PREP TIME: 10 min • TOTAL TIME: 30 min

1½ cups THRIVE® Apple Slices

2 tablespoons butter

2 tablespoons THRIVE® Brown Sugar

¼ teaspoon cinnamon

4 THRIVE® Whole Eggs, rehydrated
 (¼ cup powder + ½ cup water)

¾ cup THRIVE® White Flour

¾ cup THRIVE® Powdered Milk, rehydrated
 (2¼ tablespoons powder + ¾ cup water)

1 teaspoon vanilla extract

3 tablespoons THRIVE® White Sugar

½ teaspoon THRIVE® Iodized Salt

1 Put oven rack in middle position and preheat oven to 400°F.

2 In a medium-sized bowl, cover apples with warm water. Let sit for 5-10 minutes until softened and rehydrated. Drain.

3 In a sauté pan, sauté rehydrated apple slices with butter, brown sugar, and cinnamon until tender.

4 In a blender or food processor, whip eggs, flour, milk, vanilla, white sugar, and salt on high for 1 minute.

5 Transfer hot apples to a greased 8 x 8 x 2 inch baking dish. Pour batter over apples. Bake for 15-20 minutes. Top with powdered sugar and maple syrup, if desired.

 Tip *from the* Kitchen

You can make a variation of this recipe by swapping the THRIVE® Apple Slices for THRIVE® Peach Slices.

WHOLE WHEAT CREPES

With crepes, the possibilities for a perfect meal or dessert are endless.

SERVES 8 • PREP TIME: 30 min • TOTAL TIME: 40 min

1½ cups THRIVE® Whole Wheat Flour

6 THRIVE® Whole Eggs, rehydrated
(6 tablespoons powder + ¾ cup water)

2½ cups THRIVE® Powdered Milk, rehydrated
(7 ½ tablespoons powder + 2 ½ cups water)

2 tablespoons THRIVE® White Sugar

¼ teaspoon THRIVE® Iodized Salt

2 teaspoons vanilla extract

½ cup butter, melted

1 In a blender or a large mixing bowl, mix all ingredients together until smooth. Let mixture stand for 15 minutes in the refrigerator.

2 Heat a skillet or crepe pan over medium-high heat. Wipe a small amount of butter or oil over the skillet (adding too much will cause your crepes to fall apart).

3 Add ¼ cup of batter to the bottom of the skillet and tilt the pan making sure the entire surface is covered. Cook until the edges appear dry and the batter is set in the center. Flip once and cook for an additional 10-15 seconds. With a spatula, gently lift the crepe from the skillet and set aside. Repeat for additional servings. Fill your crepes with fresh fruits or vegetables. The berry compote on page 37 also makes a great filling. Any unused crepes may be frozen.

GERMADE WITH BERRY PURÉE & CREAM

This warm breakfast cereal is so nutritious and filling – it will start your day out right.

SERVES 2 • PREP TIME: 15 min • TOTAL TIME: 15 min

2 cups THRIVE® Powdered Milk, rehydrated
(1 tablespoon powder + 2 cups water)

½ cup THRIVE® Germade

½ teaspoon vanilla

1 teaspoon THRIVE® Brown Sugar

1 cup THRIVE® berries *(any variety)*

½ cup THRIVE® Apple Drink
(1 tablespoon powder + ½ cup water)

1-2 tablespoons THRIVE® White Sugar

whipped cream or yogurt, *optional*

cinnamon, *optional*

1 Heat prepared milk until just before boiling, then reduce heat. Add in germade, stirring constantly until thickened and adding more milk if it becomes too thick. Add vanilla and brown sugar; stir.

2 Place rehydrated berries and juice in a food processor or blender. Add sugar and pulse until smooth and creamy. Stores well in refrigerator and freezes as well.

3 Top germade with berry purée and whipped cream or yogurt, if desired.

HOMEMADE CORNBREAD

This southern basic will become a family favorite. The warm and rich texture will always make you feel at home.

SERVES 12 • PREP TIME: 15 min • TOTAL TIME: 45 min

½ cup butter, melted

1 cup THRIVE® White Sugar

2 THRIVE® Whole Eggs, rehydrated
  (2 tablespoons powder + 4 tablespoons water)

1 cup buttermilk *or 3 tablespoons THRIVE® Powdered Milk +
  1 cup water + 1 tablespoon vinegar or lemon juice*

½ teaspoon THRIVE® Baking Soda

1 cup THRIVE® Cornmeal

1 cup THRIVE® White Flour

½ teaspoon THRIVE® Iodized Salt

1 Preheat oven to 325°F.

2 In a mixing bowl, whisk together melted butter and sugar. Add prepared eggs and prepared buttermilk and continue to whisk.

3 Combine dry ingredients in a separate bowl, mixing thoroughly; add to the wet ingredients. Stir until combined, but do not over-mix.

4 Pour batter into a greased muffin pan or 8 x 8 inch baking dish. Bake for 20-30 minutes or until inserted toothpick comes out clean.

THRIVE® FOODS

Cornmeal
White Flour
♻ Powdered Milk
♻ Whole Eggs
White Sugar
Baking Soda
Salt

♻ - May be exchanged for fresh ingredients.

PINTO BEAN BREAD

This flavorful bread is a great way to add variety to your choice of grains.

SERVES 20 • PREP TIME: 2 hours 30 min • TOTAL TIME: 3 hours 30 min

2   cups THRIVE® Instant Milk, rehydrated
    (¾ cup powder + 2 cups water)
2   tablespoons yeast
2   cups THRIVE® Pinto Beans, cooked, puréed, and unseasoned
2   tablespoons THRIVE® Iodized Salt
2   tablespoons THRIVE® White Sugar
2   tablespoons shortening
6   cups THRIVE® White Flour

1 In a small saucepan, scald prepared milk.

2 Pour milk into a large bowl and allow to cool until warm. Stir in yeast until completely dissolved.

3 Blend in beans, salt, sugar, and shortening, then add flour. Knead until smooth and elastic.

4 Place into a greased bowl, then cover the bowl with plastic wrap. Let the dough rise until it has doubled in size.

5 Divide dough into two equal portions and shape into loaves. Place each portion into a greased loaf pan and let rise until it has doubled again.

6 Bake at 350°F for 50 minutes.

 Tip *from the* **Kitchen**

Directions for properly rinsing and cooking beans can be found on page 13.

FEATHER ROLLS

These rolls are so light and fluffy that you will never be able to eat just one.

SERVES 30 (5 dozen rolls) • PREP TIME: 30 min • TOTAL TIME: 1 hour

7 cups THRIVE® Whole Wheat Flour, divided
2 cups THRIVE® White Flour
2 tablespoons dry yeast
1 cup THRIVE® Powdered Milk, dry
3 cups warm water
1 cup vegetable oil
½ cup honey or sugar
4 THRIVE® Whole Eggs, rehydrated
   (4 tablespoons powder + ½ cup water)
2 teaspoons THRIVE® Iodized Salt
   extra cups of THRIVE® White Flour

1 In a large mixing bowl, mix 5 cups whole wheat flour, yeast, and dry milk. Add water, oil, and honey, and mix well for 1-2 minutes. Cover and let dough rest for 10 minutes, allowing the yeast to become active.

2 Add remaining 2 cups of whole wheat flour, along with eggs and salt; mix. Add white flour, 1 cup at a time, until dough begins to pull away from the sides of the bowl. Knead for 5-6 minutes. Dough should be soft and manageable. (Stiff dough produces dry, heavy rolls, so if dough stiffens while mixing, drizzle a little warm water over as you knead it.)

3 Dough may be used immediately or stored for several days in the refrigerator. If using immediately, lightly oil hands and counter top; shape or roll out into rolls. Cover loosely and allow to rise until very light. Bake rolls at 350°F for 18-20 minutes.

30 MINUTE ROLLS

Because these rolls come together so quickly, they can be made any night of the week.

SERVES 12 • PREP TIME: 15 min • TOTAL TIME: 30 min

3½ cups warm water
6 tablespoons instant yeast
1 cup vegetable oil
¾ cup THRIVE® White Sugar
1 tablespoon THRIVE® Iodized Salt
3 THRIVE® Whole Eggs, rehydrated
   (3 tablespoons powder + 6 tablespoons water)
3 tablespoons additional water
8 cups THRIVE® White Flour

1 Preheat oven to 400°F.

2 Use a mixer to combine warm water, instant yeast, oil, and granulated sugar. Let activate 5 minutes until bubbly.

3 Add remaining ingredients to bubbling mixture. Mix well and roll out on well-floured surface. Form dough into rolls and let rise approximately 15 minutes.

4 Bake for 10-12 minutes until golden brown. Cool and serve.

Breads & Grains

SUN-DRIED TOMATO FOCACCIA

Try serving this focaccia recipe alongside dinner with any of your favorite toppings.

SERVES 12 • PREP TIME: 20 min • TOTAL TIME: 45 min

1 cup warm water
1 tablespoon active dry yeast
1 tablespoon THRIVE® White Sugar
1 teaspoon THRIVE® Iodized Salt
1 tablespoon olive oil
2 cups THRIVE® White Flour
½ cup THRIVE® Whole Wheat Flour
10 oz. sun-dried tomatoes packed in oil
1½ teaspoons Italian Herbs
¾ cup shredded Parmesan cheese
2 THRIVE® Whole Eggs, rehydrated
   (2 tablespoons powder + ¼ cup water)
   THRIVE® Iodized Salt and pepper

1 Preheat oven to 400°F.

2 In a medium-sized mixing bowl, combine water, yeast, and sugar. Let stand for 5 minutes until activated and bubbly. Add salt, oil, and enough flour to make the dough come together. Knead until smooth and elastic.

3 Roll dough into a rectangle and place on a 9 x 13 inch baking sheet that has been greased. Press dough with hands to edges filling in all of the corners. Make indentations all over the surface of the dough. Brush the dough generously with the oil from the drained sun-dried tomatoes. Sprinkle the Italian Herbs over the dough evenly and top with the drained, chopped sun-dried tomatoes.

4 In another bowl, combine cheese, prepared eggs, ½ teaspoon oil from the drained sun-dried tomatoes. Whisk together and pour over the dough distributing mixture evenly. Generously season with salt and pepper.

5 Bake for 15-20 minutes or until edges are golden brown. Divide into squares before serving.

Breads & Grains

↻ - May be exchanged for fresh ingredients.

ITALIAN BREADSTICKS

Adding whole wheat flour adds flavor and a boost of nutrition. This recipe also works as a pizza dough base.

SERVES 12 • PREP TIME: 30 min • TOTAL TIME: 1 hour 30 min

¼ cup warm water
2¼ teaspoons active dry yeast *(1 package)*
2 tablespoons THRIVE® White Sugar
3 cups THRIVE® White Flour
1¼ cups THRIVE® Whole Wheat Flour
2 tablespoons butter, melted and cooled
2 teaspoons THRIVE® Iodized Salt
1½ cups warm water

Topping (brush over breadsticks):
3 tablespoons butter, melted
½ teaspoon THRIVE® Iodized Salt
½ teaspoon Italian seasoning
¼ teaspoon garlic powder

1 Place ¼ cup warm water in the bowl of a mixer, sprinkle in the yeast and sugar and set aside until activated and bubbly (about 5 minutes). Slowly mix in the flour, butter and salt, alternating with the 1½ cups warm water. Mix with paddle attachment until a slightly sticky baller forms and pulls away from the sides of the bowl (about 5 minutes).

2 Knead the dough by hand on a well-floured surface until very smooth and soft. Roll into a 2 foot long log, cut into twelve 1½ inch wide pieces. Knead each piece slightly and shape into a 7 inch long bread stick. Arrange 2 inches apart on a greased baking sheet. Cover with a cloth, let rise until almost doubled (about 45 minutes).

3 Preheat oven to 400°F. Brush the bread sticks with ½ the melted butter then sprinkle with ¼ teaspoon salt. Bake until golden brown (about 15 minutes). Meanwhile mix the remaining salt with the Italian seasoning and garlic powder.

4 When you take the breadsticks out of the oven brush with remaining melted butter, salt, and Italian seasoning mixture.

PIZZA DOUGH

Making your own pizza dough is so fun because you can add all of your favorite sauces and toppings to make the pizza just how you like it.

SERVES 10 • PREP TIME: 15 min • TOTAL TIME: 2 hours 30 min

1 tablespoon active dry yeast
1¼ cups warm water
2 tablespoons vegetable oil
4 cups THRIVE® White Flour
1 teaspoon THRIVE® Iodized Salt

1 In a large bowl, dissolve yeast in warm water. Let sit for a few minutes. Stir in oil. In a separate bowl, sift together flour and salt. Incorporate into the liquid mixture.

2 Knead dough on a lightly floured surface until it is smooth and elastic (about 15 minutes). Shape into a ball; place in a greased bowl, turning over once. Cover with a cloth and let rise until doubled (about 2 hours).

3 Punch dough down; divide it in half. Roll out on two pizza pans. Bake at 425°F for 11 minutes.

WHOLE WHEAT PITA BREAD

With this simple recipe you will never need to buy packaged pita bread again.

SERVES 10 • PREP TIME: 20 min • TOTAL TIME: 1 hour 30 min

2¼ teaspoons active dry yeast *(1 package)*
1 tablespoon THRIVE® White Sugar *or honey*
1¼ cups warm water
1 cup THRIVE® Whole Wheat Flour
2 cups THRIVE® White Flour
1½ teaspoons THRIVE® Iodized Salt
2 tablespoons olive oil

1 In a large mixing bowl, dissolve yeast and sugar in warm water. Let sit 5 minutes to activate. Mix in flour, salt, and olive oil and mix well to form a soft dough.

2 Knead the dough for approximately 10 minutes, or until dough is smooth and elastic. Place dough in a bowl that has been lightly coated with oil and cover with plastic wrap or a damp kitchen towel. Set aside to double in size; approximately 45 minutes to an hour.

3 When it has doubled in size, punch the dough down to release some of the trapped gases and divide it into 10 pieces. Roll each piece into a ball, cover the balls with a damp kitchen towel, and let them rest for 10 minutes. This step allows the dough to relax so that it will be easier to shape.

4 Preheat oven to 500°F.
On a floured surface, roll each ball into a 5-6 inch circle, about ¼ inch thick. Dust with flour on both sides to prevent sticking. Transfer to a greased baking sheet and allow to rise 10 minutes, or until slightly raised.

5 Bake on the bottom rack of the oven for 4-6 minutes until they are puffed up and golden brown.

- May be exchanged for fresh ingredients.

WHOLE WHEAT TORTILLAS

Have a little Mexican fiesta with these healthy and delicious tortillas.

SERVES 20 • PREP TIME: 10 min • TOTAL TIME: 1 hour 20 min

1 cup THRIVE® White Flour
4 cups THRIVE® Whole Wheat Flour
2 teaspoons THRIVE® Iodized Salt
½ cup shortening
2¼ cups boiling water
    additional flour for rolling

1 Sift together white flour, whole wheat flour, and salt. Add shortening with fork, pastry cutter or hands and mix until crumbly.

2 Make a well in the center of the mixture, then pour boiling water in the well. Mix with a fork until all of the water is evenly incorporated into the mixture. Dough should be soft and not sticky. If your dough is too flaky, add more water 2 tablespoons at a time until dough comes together.

3 Sprinkle with a bit of additional flour and knead until the dough does not stick to fingers. Make balls the size of golf balls and place them on a sheet pan. Cover the dough with a cloth and let sit for an hour.

4 Heat a griddle or large frying pan over high heat. On a lightly floured surface, roll out a tortilla as thinly as you prefer. Fry the first side for approximately 10 seconds until you see a bubble form in the middle of the tortilla. Flip the tortilla and let it cook for approximately 30 additional seconds. Flip the tortilla once more and let it cook for 30 seconds more.

MAIN DISHES

One cannot think well, love well, sleep well, if one has not dined well.

Virginia Woolf

CAULIFLOWER CHEESE SOUP

This creamy soup will warm your heart and home.

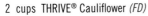

SERVES 4 • PREP TIME: 20 min • TOTAL TIME: 1 hour

2 cups THRIVE® Cauliflower *(FD)*

¼ cup THRIVE® Chopped Onions *(FD)*

¼ cup THRIVE® Carrot Dices

¼ cup THRIVE® Celery *(FD)*

4 cups THRIVE® chicken broth
   (4 teaspoons THRIVE® Chicken Bouillon + 4 cups water)

2 cups heavy cream

½ teaspoon Worcestershire sauce

1 cup THRIVE® Shredded Cheddar Cheese
   THRIVE® Iodized Salt and pepper to taste
   chopped chives for garnish

1 In a small bowl, cover Cheddar cheese with warm water. Let sit 5-10 minutes until softened and rehydrated. Drain.

2 Combine cauliflower, onions, carrots, celery, and chicken broth in a slow cooker. Cover and cook on high heat for 45 minutes to 1 hour. Alternately, you may simmer the ingredients on the stove until all of the vegetables are soft and cooked through.

3 Transfer soup to a blender and purée.

4 Return mixture to stove top or slow cooker and blend in cream, Worcestershire sauce, cheese, and desired salt and pepper.

5 Ladle soup into bowls and serve. Garnish with cheese and chives, if desired.

CORN CHOWDER

Thrive® Sweet Corn is one of my favorite ingredients to work with. This corn chowder highlights it's fantastic flavor and is an excellent option for lunch or dinner.

SERVES 6 • PREP TIME: 15 min • TOTAL TIME: 1 hour

4 tablespoons butter
3 tablespoons THRIVE® White Flour
½ cup THRIVE® Chopped Onions *(FD)*
3 cups water
2 cups THRIVE® Potato Dices *(FD)*
1 cup THRIVE® Sweet Corn *(FD)*
¼ cup THRIVE® Celery *(FD)*
1 can creamed corn
2 tablespoons THRIVE® White Sugar
2 teaspoons THRIVE® Iodized Salt
2 teaspoons ground black pepper
3 cups half and half cream
¼ cup THRIVE® Chopped Spinach *(FD), optional*

1 Melt butter in a large pot over medium heat. Whisk in flour until thick and bubbly (about 2 minutes).

2 Rehydrate onions in water. Once rehydrated, drain excess liquid. Add rehydrated onions to the butter and sauté until translucent.

3 Add water, potatoes, corn, celery, creamed corn, sugar, salt and pepper. Whisk until smooth. Cover and simmer until potatoes and vegetables are tender (about 30 minutes).

4 Add half and half and simmer uncovered until soup has thickened to a creamy consistency (about 15 minutes).

5 Season to taste with additional salt and pepper if needed. If desired, add spinach during last several minutes, just before serving.

Main Dishes

CREAMY CHICKEN NOODLE SOUP WITH DUMPLINGS

Our Thrive® Creamy Chicken Noodle Soup is excellent on its own and even better when adding dumplings. The cornmeal dumplings make this soup a meal by adding a hearty texture and flavor.

SERVES 6 • PREP TIME: 5 min • TOTAL TIME: 30 min

Soup:
- 2 tablespoons butter
- ½ cup THRIVE® Carrot Dices
- ½ cup THRIVE® Celery *(FD)*
- 2 cups THRIVE® Creamy Chicken Noodle Soup mix
- 1 cup THRIVE® Chopped Chicken *(FD)*

Dumplings:
- 1 cup THRIVE® White Flour
- ½ cup THRIVE® Whole Wheat Flour
- 2 teaspoons THRIVE® Baking Powder
- ½ cup THRIVE® Cornmeal
- 1 tablespoon THRIVE® White Sugar
- 1 teaspoon THRIVE® Iodized Salt
- ¾ cup THRIVE® Instant Milk, rehydrated
  (4 ½ tablespoons powder + ¾ cup water)

1 Bring 6 cups water to a boil. Add butter, carrots, celery and chicken in addition to 2 cups soup mix. Stir until combined and simmer for 5-10 minutes.

If using fresh vegetables, melt butter in large saucepan. Sauté diced carrots and celery until soft. Add 6 cups water and bring to a boil. Add 2 cups soup mix and stir until combined, simmer for 5-10 minutes.

For Dumplings:

1 In a large bowl combine flour, baking powder, cornmeal, sugar, and salt. Add the prepared milk and mix just until combined; mixture should be thick. Drop 12 tablespoons of dumpling mixture into simmering soup. Cover and simmer for another 12 minutes.

SLOW COOKED 3 BEAN CHILI

Chili is one of the best ways to utilize your Thrive® ingredients.
It's a hearty meal all wrapped up into one dish.

SERVES 6 • PREP TIME: 10 min • TOTAL TIME: 4-8 hours

¼ cup THRIVE® Chopped Onions

4 cloves garlic, minced

1 tablespoon chili powder

1 tablespoon cumin

¼ cup THRIVE® Tomato Powder

4 teaspoons THRIVE® Chicken Bouillon

2 cans (14.5 oz) diced tomatoes

1 cup THRIVE® Black Beans, rinsed and drained

1 cup THRIVE® Small White Navy Beans, rinsed and drained

1 cup THRIVE® Kidney Beans, rinsed and drained

2 cans (4 oz) diced green chiles

6 cups water

2 cups THRIVE® Ground Beef

2 cups THRIVE® Shredded Cheddar Cheese

½ cup THRIVE® Sour Cream, prepared

1 In a 3½ to 6-quart slow cooker place the onion, garlic, chili powder, cumin, tomato powder, chicken bouillon, canned tomatoes, beans, green chiles, water, and ground beef. Stir to combine.

2 Cover and cook on low heat for 7 to 8 hours or on high-heat setting for 3½ to 4 hours. Stir in the cheese until melted.

3 Ladle the chili into 6 bowls. If desired, top with sour cream and additional cheese.

Tip *from the* Kitchen

For instructions on how to prepare THRIVE® Sour Cream, refer to page 11.

CREAMY & CHEESY POTATO SOUP

Add Creamy Potato Soup to your dinner line up as a side dish or make it the main event by adding diced bacon.

SERVES 4 • PREP TIME: 15 min • TOTAL TIME: 15 min

3 cups THRIVE® chicken broth *(3 teaspoons THRIVE® Chicken Bouillon + 3 cups water)*

1 tablespoon THRIVE® Chopped Onions

1 cup THRIVE® Potato Dices *(FD)*

2 tablespoons butter

2 tablespoons THRIVE® White Flour

¼ teaspoon THRIVE® Iodized Salt

1 teaspoon black pepper

1 cup THRIVE® Instant Milk , rehydrated *(6 tablespoons powder + 1 cup water)*

¾ cup THRIVE® Shredded Cheddar Cheese
THRIVE® Iodized Salt and pepper to taste

1 In a mixing bowl, cover Cheddar cheese with warm water. Let sit 5-10 minutes until softened and rehydrated. Drain.

2 In a large saucepan, combine chicken broth, onion, and potatoes. Bring to a boil and simmer for 5-10 minutes or until potatoes are tender.

3 Remove from heat and carefully ladle ½ soup mixture into blender or food processor. Cover and blend until smooth. (You could also use an immersion/stick blender). Repeat with remaining soup and set aside.

4 In the same saucepan, melt the butter. Whisk in flour, salt, and pepper. Slowly add prepared milk while whisking. Cook and stir until mixture is thickened and bubbly. Stir in the blended vegetable mixture and Cheddar cheese. Cook and stir until soup is heated through. Season to taste with additional salt and pepper.

MEXICAN TAMALE PIE

My favorite part of this dish is the cornmeal. It adds a rich and hearty texture that makes this an ideal dinner option for the whole family.

SERVES 6 • PREP TIME: 15 min • TOTAL TIME: 1 hour

1½ cups THRIVE® Instant Milk, rehydrated
    (9 tablespoons powder + 1½ cups water)

1 cup THRIVE® Cornmeal

1 THRIVE® Whole Egg, rehydrated
   (1 tablespoon powder + 2 tablespoons water)

1 tablespoon vegetable oil

1 medium onion, chopped *or THRIVE® Chopped Onions, rehydrated (⅓ cup onions + ⅓ cup water)*

1 (10 oz) can enchilada sauce

1 (14.5 oz) can diced tomatoes, undrained

1 cup THRIVE® Sweet Corn *(FD)*

2 cups THRIVE® Taco TVP *or 2 cups THRIVE® Cooked Beef, Ground + 1 tablespoon taco seasoning*

1½ cups THRIVE® Shredded Monterey Jack Cheese

1 In a small bowl, cover corn with warm water and let sit 5-10 minutes until softened or rehydrated. Drain. In another bowl, repeat same process if using beef TVP.

2 Preheat oven to 350°F.

3 In a large bowl combine prepared milk, cornmeal, and prepared egg. Set aside.

4 Heat oil in a large skillet. Sauté onion until translucent. Add enchilada sauce, diced tomatoes, and corn. Simmer over medium heat for 4 minutes. Add rehydrated meat and simmer for 1 minute.

5 Stir sauce mixture into cornmeal mixture and pour into a greased 2 ½ quart casserole dish. Bake for 45 to 50 minutes.

6 Sprinkle with grated cheese and bake until cheese is melted. Garnish with sour cream and green onions, if desired.

- May be exchanged for fresh ingredients.

BEEF STROGANOFF

The Thrive® Mushrooms and Roast Beef are a perfect combination in this savory Russian classic.

SERVES 4 • PREP TIME: 15 min • TOTAL TIME: 15 min

4 cups THRIVE® Egg Noodles
2 cups THRIVE® Roast Beef *(FD)*
2 cups THRIVE® Mushroom Pieces *(FD)*
2 tablespoons butter
1 (15 oz) can cream of mushroom soup
3 tablespoons THRIVE® Sour Cream Powder, dry
1½ cups THRIVE® Instant Milk, rehydrated
  (9 tablespoons powder + 1½ cups water)
2 teaspoons paprika
2 tablespoons Worcestershire sauce

1 Bring salted water to a boil and cook egg noodles according to package directions.

2 In a medium-sized bowl, add freeze-dried roast beef and cover with warm water. Let sit for 5-10 minutes or until softened and rehydrated. Drain. In another medium size bowl, repeat same process with mushroom pieces.

3 In a large sauté pan, melt butter and add rehydrated roast beef. Sauté for 1 minute. Add rehydrated mushroom pieces and sauté for an additional minute.

4 In a separate bowl mix the soup, sour cream powder, milk, paprika, and Worcestershire sauce. Pour over mushroom and beef mixture in sauté pan and mix together.

5 Heat through and pour over cooked noodles.

Main Dishes

SWEET & SOUR MEATBALLS

You will think you are at a Hawaiian barbeque when you taste this sweet and spicy dish.

SERVES 10 • PREP TIME: 20 min • TOTAL TIME: 45 min

2 cups THRIVE® Cooked Beef, Ground
½ cup dry bread crumbs
¼ cup THRIVE® Powdered Milk, rehydrated
   (¾ tablespoon powder + ¼ cup water)
2 tablespoons THRIVE® Chopped Onions *(FD)*
1 teaspoon THRIVE® Iodized Salt
½ teaspoon Worcestershire sauce
1 THRIVE® Whole Egg, rehydrated
   (1 tablespoon powder + 2 tablespoons water)
½ cup THRIVE® Brown Sugar, packed
1 tablespoon cornstarch
1 (20 oz) can pineapple tidbits with juice
⅓ cup vinegar
1 tablespoon soy sauce
⅛ cup THRIVE® Mixed Bell Peppers
5 cups THRIVE® White Rice, prepared

1 Rehydrate freeze-dried meat by bringing 4 cups water to a boil. Add beef and boil for 5 minutes. Drain excess water.

2 Mix meat, dry bread crumbs, milk, onions, salt, Worcestershire sauce, and egg together; shape into twenty 1½ inch sized balls.

3 Place in skillet and cook over medium heat, turning occasionally, until brown (about 20 minutes).

— OR —

Bake in an ungreased 9 x 13 inch pan at 400°F for 20-25 minutes, until light brown.

4 Mix brown sugar and cornstarch in a skillet. Stir in pineapple, juice, vinegar, and soy sauce.

5 Heat to boiling, stirring occasionally. Reduce heat to medium, then add meatballs and peppers.

6 Cover and let simmer, stirring occasionally, for 10-15 minutes. Serve over cooked rice.

BEEF ENCHILADA BAKE

This simple recipe is like a Mexican fiesta in a pan!

SERVES 6 • PREP TIME: 15 min • TOTAL TIME: 30 min

1 cup THRIVE® Cooked Beef, Ground *(FD)*
  or 1 cup THRIVE® Beef TVP

1 (10 ¾ oz) can condensed tomato soup

1 cup salsa

1 cup THRIVE® Sweet Corn *(FD)*

6 corn tortillas, cut into 1-inch squares

1 cup THRIVE® Shredded Cheddar Cheese
  optional toppings: sour cream, olives, diced tomatoes

Tip *from the* Kitchen

Try preparing our THRIVE® Sour Cream
Powder as a topping.

1 Preheat oven to 350°F.

2 In a large bowl, cover freeze-dried ground beef or TVP with warm water. Let sit for 5-10 minutes until softened and rehydrated. Drain. Repeat the same process for corn and cheese.

3 In a large skillet, combine ground beef, tomato soup, salsa, corn, and tortillas; heat through. Transfer to a 2½ quart baking dish and top with cheese.

4 Bake for 15 minutes or until cheese is bubbly. Top each serving with olives and a dollop of sour cream, if desired.

TVP TACOS

These tacos make a great vegetarian Mexican dinner.

SERVES 6 • PREP TIME: 20 min • TOTAL TIME: 20 min

2 cups THRIVE® Taco TVP
*or 2 cups THRIVE® Beef TVP
+ 1 tablespoon taco seasoning*

2 tablespoons olive or vegetable oil

2 tablespoons THRIVE® Mixed Bell Peppers

1 cup salsa

6 flour tortillas or hard taco shells

optional toppings: tomato, cheese, lettuce, olives, sour cream

1 In a large skillet, heat water over medium heat. Add the TVP, stirring well. Allow the TVP to rehydrate for 2-3 minutes. Remove excess water.

2 Add oil to TVP. Next, add peppers and taco seasoning (if applicable); stir well. Continue cooking for an additional 3-5 minutes, stirring frequently.

3 Mix in salsa and remove from heat. Serve with toppings in tortillas or shells.

Tip *from the* **Kitchen**

Try our Whole Wheat Tortilla recipe on page 53.

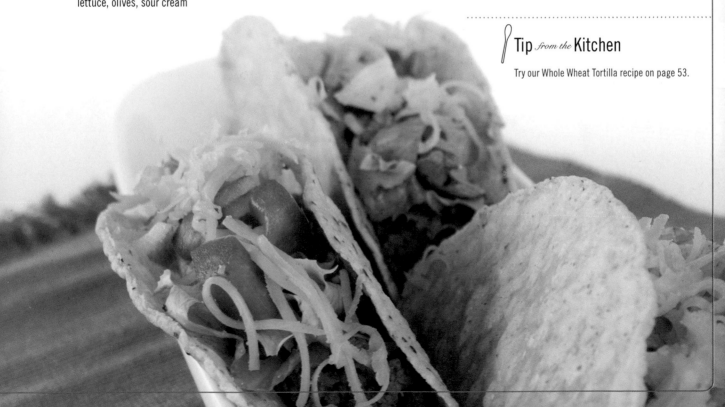

CHICKEN SALAD SANDWICH

These sandwiches are ideal for outdoor picnics.

SERVES 4 • PREP TIME: 10 min • TOTAL TIME: 25 min

1½ cups THRIVE® Chopped Chicken *(FD)*
½ cup THRIVE® Celery *(FD)*
⅓ cup THRIVE® Chopped Onion *(FD)*
3 cups water
½ cup mayonnaise
 THRIVE® Iodized Salt and pepper to taste

1 Combine chicken, celery, onion, and water in a saucepan over high heat. Bring to a boil and reduce heat to low and simmer until mixture is rehydrated (about 10 minutes). Put the mixture into a colander and let the water drain for another 10 minutes. Set aside in the refrigerator until cool.

2 Combine the cooled chicken mixture with mayonnaise. Season the chicken mixture with salt and pepper to taste. Spoon onto rolls or croissants.

Tip *from the* **Kitchen**

For an extra dash of flavor, try adding 1 tablespoon of prepared pesto sauce.

MACARONI & CHEESE

Enjoy a bowl of mom's made-with-love Mac & Cheese.

SERVES 4 • PREP TIME: 15 min • TOTAL TIME: 15 min

¾ cup THRIVE® Cheese Blend

2 tablespoons THRIVE® Butter Powder, dry

1½ cups THRIVE® Instant Milk, rehydrated
   (9 tablespoons powder + 1½ cups water)

3 cups THRIVE® Elbow Macaroni

1 Cook pasta in boiling water until soft.

2 Combine cheese blend, butter powder, and milk in a saucepan over medium heat.

3 Add cooked macaroni to the saucepan, stirring until noodles are coated.

SHEPHERD'S PIE

Wrap dinner up into one dish with this fantastic Shepherd's Pie recipe. The bold flavors in this dish will please everyone at the table.

SERVES 12 • PREP TIME: 15 min • TOTAL TIME: 45 min

- 2 tablespoons butter
- 1 medium onion, chopped *or THRIVE® Chopped Onions, rehydrated (⅓ cup onions + ⅓ cup water)*
- 2 cups THRIVE® Cooked Roast Beef *(FD)*
- 1 tablespoon THRIVE® White Flour
- 1 teaspoon THRIVE® Beef Bouillon
- 1 cup water
- ½ cup THRIVE® Green Peas *(FD)*
- ½ cup THRIVE® Carrot Dices
- 1 tablespoon Worcestershire sauce
- 1 teaspoon THRIVE® Iodized Salt
- 1 teaspoon ground black pepper
- 2 cups THRIVE® Potato Beads, prepared and divided
- 1 cup THRIVE® Shredded Cheddar Cheese *(FD)*

1 In a medium-sized bowl, cover roast beef with warm water. Let sit 5-10 minutes or until softened and rehydrated. Drain. In another medium-sized bowl, repeat process for cheese.

2 Preheat oven to 375°F.

3 In a large skillet, melt butter over medium heat. Sauté onions until translucent. Add rehydrated beef and sauté for 1 minute. Sprinkle beef and onions with flour and stir. Add water and beef bouillon and mix; bring to a boil. Reduce heat to low, add peas, carrots, Worcestershire sauce, salt and pepper. Mix together.

4 Simmer uncovered for 5 minutes. Grease a 9 x13 inch baking dish or pie plate. Pour filling into dish. Top with 1 cup of prepared mashed potatoes and spread evenly over top. Sprinkle with cheese.

5 Bake for 25 to 30 minutes until bubbling and brown. Top with remaining mashed potatoes and additional Cheddar cheese, if desired. Serve warm.

CHICKEN POT PIE

Chicken Pot Pie has always been one of my favorite dishes to make. I gave this recipe a twist by making a delicious crust using Thrive® 6 Grain Pancake Mix.

SERVES 12-14, yields 2 pies • PREP TIME: 25 min • TOTAL TIME: 1 hour

2 cups THRIVE® Chopped Chicken *(FD)*
1 cup THRIVE® Carrot Dices
1 cup THRIVE® Green Peas *(FD)*
½ cup THRIVE® Celery *(FD)*
⅓ cup butter
⅓ cup onion, diced
⅓ cup THRIVE® White Flour
½ teaspoon THRIVE® Iodized Salt
½ teaspoon black pepper
½ teaspoon celery seed
1¾ cups THRIVE® chicken broth *(1¾ teaspoons THRIVE® Chicken Bouillon + 1¾ cups water)*
⅔ cup THRIVE® Instant Milk, rehydrated *(4 tablespoons powder + ⅔ cup water)*

Pie Crust (can replace using regular pie crust):
4 cups THRIVE® 6 Grain Pancake Mix
4 tablespoons butter, melted
1½ cups THRIVE® Instant Milk, rehydrated *(9 tablespoons powder + 1½ cups water)*

1 Preheat oven to 350°F.

2 In a saucepan, combine chicken, carrots, peas, and celery. Cover with water and bring to a boil, then simmer for 15 minutes. Remove from heat, drain, and set aside.

3 In the saucepan over medium heat, cook onions in butter until soft and translucent. Stir in flour, salt, pepper, and celery seed. Slowly stir in chicken broth and milk. Simmer over medium-low heat until thick. Remove from heat and combine with chicken mixture.

For pie crust:

1 In a large bowl, stir 6 Grain Pancake Mix, butter, and milk until a soft dough forms. On well floured surface, work dough and shape into a ball; knead 5 times. Divide dough into 4 equal segments.

2 Gently press dough segment into bottom of pie plate and up the sides. Place ½ the chicken and sauce mixture in bottom of pie crust. Cover with another dough segment and seal edges. Make several small slits in the top to allow steam to escape. Assemble second pie with remaining ingredients.

3 Bake in the preheated oven for 15 to 20 minutes, or until dough is golden brown and filling is bubbly. Cool for 10 minutes before serving.

WHOLE WHEAT MEATLOAF

While I was growing up, my mom always made delicious meatloaf. This recipe reminds me so much of the love and hard work that goes into making a home-cooked meal.

SERVES 8 • PREP TIME: 15 min • TOTAL TIME: 1 hour 15 min

2½ cups THRIVE® Cooked Beef, Ground *(FD)*

1 cup THRIVE® Hard White Winter Wheat, cooked

2 THRIVE® Whole Eggs, rehydrated
(2 tablespoons powder + ¼ cup water)

1 cup THRIVE® Instant Milk, rehydrated
(6 tablespoons powder + 1 cup water)

¼ cup THRIVE® Chopped Onions *(FD)*

¼ cup THRIVE® Mixed Bell Peppers

2½ teaspoons THRIVE® Iodized Salt

¼ teaspoon black pepper

1 teaspoon sage

1 teaspoon Worcestershire sauce

1 teaspoon mustard

5 tablespoons THRIVE® Brown Sugar

¼ cup ketchup

¼ teaspoon nutmeg

1 teaspoon dry mustard

1 Wash 1 cup of hard white winter wheat. Combine wheat with 6 cups of cold water in a large pot. Bring to a boil. Turn heat to low and simmer for 1 hour and 45 minutes, stirring occasionally. Drain excess water from wheat.

2 Rehydrate ground beef in a large bowl by covering with warm water. Let sit for 5-10 minutes until softened and rehydrated.

3 Preheat oven to 350°F.

4 Combine first 11 ingredients in a large bowl (ground beef through prepared mustard) and place into loaf pan.

5 Combine remaining ingredients and spread over meatloaf.

6 Bake for 1 hour.

Main Dishes

CHICKEN VEGETABLE CASSEROLE

Casseroles are great for feeding a large family or group of friends, and this one will give "casserole" a whole new meaning.

SERVES 4 • PREP TIME: 15 min • TOTAL TIME: 50 min

1 cup THRIVE® Chopped Chicken *(FD)*
4 cups THRIVE® Egg Noodle Pasta
½ cup THRIVE® Sweet Corn *(FD)*
½ cup THRIVE® Celery *(FD)*
½ cup THRIVE® Carrot Dices
1 tablespoon THRIVE® Chopped Onions *(FD)*
1 teaspoon THRIVE® Iodized Salt
1 teaspoon garlic powder
1 teaspoon dried thyme
2 cups THRIVE® Gravy *(recipe on page 93)*
¼ cup THRIVE® Powdered Milk, rehydrated
   (¾ tablespoon powder + ¼ cup water)
1 cup Parmesan cheese, shredded

1 In a small bowl, cover chicken dices with warm water. Let sit for 5-10 minutes or until softened and rehydrated. Drain.

2 Preheat oven to 350°F.

3 In a large pot of salted boiling water, cook egg noodle pasta according to the directions on the can. Toss cooked noodles, gravy, and milk in a large bowl with vegetables and onion until completely coated. Add salt, garlic powder, and thyme.

4 Toss mixture with chicken and stir to combine. Pour into casserole dish and top with ½ cup Parmesan.

5 Cover casserole with foil and bake at 350°F for 20 minutes, or until bubbly. Take off foil and top with remaining ½ cup Parmesan cheese. Bake an additional 15 minutes.

BLACK BEAN & RICE BURGERS

These are a great substitute for beef patties. You can give your burger a real boost by topping it with your favorite condiments such as guacamole, cheese, and salsa.

SERVES 4 • PREP TIME: 3 hours • TOTAL TIME: 3 hours

2 cups THRIVE® Instant White Rice, cooked
1½ cups THRIVE® Black Beans, prepared as directed
1 teaspoon chili powder
½ teaspoon cumin
¾ teaspoon THRIVE® Iodized Salt
2 cloves garlic, minced
⅓ cup white onion, chopped
2 tablespoons cilantro, chopped
1 (4 oz) can green chiles
2 tablespoons canned chipotle peppers in adobo sauce
¼ cup salsa
1 THRIVE® Whole Egg, rehydrated
  (1 tablespoon powder + 1 tablespoon water)
⅓ cup THRIVE® White Flour *extra if desired*
2 tablespoons olive oil
  slices of your favorite cheese

For Black Beans:
2 cups THRIVE® Black Beans
2 slices of bacon, *optional*
1 onion, minced
2 cloves garlic, minced
  THRIVE® Iodized Salt to taste

For Black Beans:

1 Rinse and sort beans before transferring them to a large pot or dutch oven. Cover with water and soak overnight. Alternately, use a quick soak method by heating beans until the water is boiling and then letting them sit for an hour or two. More information about beans can be found on page 13.

2 Drain beans and recover with fresh water. Add bacon, onion, salt, and garlic. Simmer over medium-low heat for a 3-5 hours, until beans are tender. Season to taste and remove bacon slices.

For Black Bean & Rice Burgers:

1 Mix rice, cooked beans, chili powder, cumin, salt, garlic, onion, cilantro, chilies, chipotle peppers, salsa, and egg in a large bowl. Mixture will be very moist.

2 Add flour, using just enough to enable you to shape the mixture into patties. Dust the outside of each patty lightly with flour.

3 Heat a medium-sized skillet over medium-high heat. Add olive oil and warm the pan. Add patties and cook until nicely browned on each side. This should take about 3-4 minutes for each side, longer if the mixture was particularly moist.

4 Top patties with your choice of cheese, reduce heat to low, and cover with lid to melt cheese. Serve with guacamole, sour cream, and salsa.

GREEN CHILE MEXICAN SOUP

This flavorful soup is more than a delicious Mexican specialty.
It also provides you with proper nutrients from beans, meats, and veggies.

SERVES 4 • PREP TIME: 20 min • TOTAL TIME: 3 hours

1 yellow onion, diced
1 pinch of THRIVE® Iodized Salt
3 cloves garlic, minced
1 can (28 oz) green chili enchilada sauce
½ jar (16 oz) salsa verde
1 can cream of chicken soup
2 cups THRIVE® chicken broth
  (2 teaspoons THRIVE® Chicken Bouillon + 2 cups water)
2 tablespoons fresh cilantro, minced
1½ cups THRIVE® Small White Navy Beans, rinsed and cooked
2 cups THRIVE® Chopped Chicken *(FD)*
1 cup THRIVE® Sweet Corn *(FD)*
½ cup THRIVE® Mixed Bell Peppers
  toppings: tortilla chips, cheese, and guacamole, as desired

1 In a large pot or slow cooker, add onions with a pinch of salt over low heat; cook until translucent.

2 Add garlic, enchilada sauce, salsa verde, cream of chicken soup, chicken broth, cilantro, pre-cooked beans, chicken, sweet corn, and bell peppers to the pot.

3 Simmer for at least 1 hour. Top with desired toppings.

Tip *from the* Kitchen

For instructions on how to properly rinse and cook beans, refer to page 13.

- May be exchanged for fresh ingredients.

TACO SOUP

You can make it as spicy or as mild as you choose simply by adding or subtracting the chili powder. No matter which way you make it, your guests will be all smiles.

SERVES 8 • PREP TIME: 20 min • TOTAL TIME: 6 hours

2 cups THRIVE® Kidney Beans, rinsed
2 cups THRIVE® Pinto Beans, rinsed
¼ cup THRIVE® Chopped Onions *(FD)*
4 tablespoons THRIVE® Tomato Powder
1 teaspoon cumin
1 tablespoon chili powder *(add 1½ teaspoons for extra heat)*
1 teaspoon dried oregano
¼ teaspoon garlic, minced
½ cup THRIVE® Taco TVP
1½ teaspoons THRIVE® Iodized Salt, divided
10½ cups water, divided
½ cup THRIVE® Mixed Bell Peppers
1 cup THRIVE® Sweet Corn *(FD)*
Sour cream, cheese, cilantro, and tortilla chips for topping, *optional*

1 In a slow cooker, combine kidney beans, pinto beans, onions, 1 teaspoon salt, and 6 cups water. Cook on high for 4 hours.

2 Stir mixture and reduce heat to low, then cook for an additional hour. Beans should now be tender. Drain, rinse, and set aside.

3 In a large pot, bring remaining 4½ cups of water to a boil. Add tomato powder, cumin, chili powder, oregano, remaining salt, and garlic. Reduce heat to medium and simmer.

4 Meanwhile, in separate bowls, rehydrate the TVP, mixed peppers, and corn, by covering with hot or boiling water. Let sit 5-10 minutes until softened and rehydrated.

5 Drain the corn, but reserve the water in the TVP and peppers. Add these three ingredients into the simmering soup. Add beans and warm through.

6 Serve hot. Garnish with sour cream, cheese, cilantro, and tortilla chips, if desired.

Tip *from the* Kitchen

For instructions on how to properly rinse and cook beans, refer to page 13.

BELL PEPPER CHICKEN

Perfect for making a quick and easy meal that looks so fancy people will think you spent hours in the kitchen!

SERVES 4 • PREP TIME: 15 min • TOTAL TIME: 30 min

- 1 cup THRIVE® Mixed Bell Peppers, rehydrated
- ½ cup Parmesan cheese, grated
- 2 THRIVE® Whole Eggs, rehydrated
  (2 tablespoons powder + ¼ cup water)
- ½ cup THRIVE® White Flour
- 2 chicken breasts
- 1 sprig rosemary *(additional for garnish, if desired)*
- 2 cups balsamic vinegar
- 1 clove garlic, minced or pressed
  THRIVE® Iodized Salt and pepper to taste

Tip *from the* Kitchen

The balsamic mixture can also be used as a great dipping sauce for breadsticks.

1 Season rehydrated eggs with salt and pepper. Preheat oven to 300°F. Preheat frying or sauté pan.

2 Combine peppers and Parmesan cheese in a small casserole dish. Gently coat chicken first in flour, then in eggs, and lastly in peppers and Parmesan mixture.

3 Add olive oil to preheated pan and place chicken breasts into pan. Reduce heat to medium, being careful not to burn the chicken breasts. After a few minutes, gently turn each breast over with a spatula. When each side is golden brown, dish breasts onto an oven safe serving plate, cover with foil, and place them in the oven at 300°F until sauce is completed (about 10 minutes).

4 Remove any large burned bits from the pan. Return pan to heat, adding the balsamic vinegar, garlic, and rosemary. Season lightly with salt. Reduce for 5-7 minutes, until slightly thickened and syrupy. Serve over chicken breasts.

REFRIED BEAN BURRITOS

My mom made refried beans from scratch all the time as I grew up. I loved how they would fill our house with the most delicious smells and I always knew that a good dinner was in the making.

SERVES 4 • PREP TIME: 15 min • TOTAL TIME: 5 hours 15 min

Beans:
- 2 cups THRIVE® Pinto Beans
- ¼ cup THRIVE® Chopped Onions
- 1 tablespoon chili powder
- 3 tablespoons cumin
- 2 teaspoons garlic powder
- 2 quarts water
  THRIVE® Iodized Salt to taste

Burritos:
- 6 flour tortillas
- 2 cups THRIVE® Shredded Cheddar Cheese, rehydrated
- ½ cup THRIVE® Sour Cream, prepared
  salsa, shredded lettuce, chopped tomatoes, sliced black olives, and sliced green onions for topping, *optional*

1 Sort beans thoroughly by removing all broken beans and any foreign objects. Soak beans overnight by submerging in water. Drain water and rinse once more before placing in slow cooker. If beans are not pre-soaked, extend cooking time to 9-10 hours.

2 Add all ingredients to slow cooker except for the salt. Cook on high 4-5 hours.

3 Drain and reserve water. Mash beans or purée in blender if you prefer. Add water as necessary to reach desired consistency. Season generously with salt and additional spices, if needed.

4 To assemble burritos: Place ½ cup warm refried beans in the center of each tortilla and top with cheese. Top with a combination of your desired toppings and roll into the shape of a burrito.

Main Dishes

83

THRIVE® FOODS

- ♻ Sweet Corn
- ♻ Bell Peppers
- ♻ Onions
- ♻ Cheddar Cheese
  Pinto Beans
- ♻ Ground Beef
  Iodized Salt

PIONEER STEW

*This thick and hearty stew is
perfect for cold winter days.*

SERVES 8 • PREP TIME: 15 min • TOTAL TIME: 1 hour 45 min

1¼ cups dry THRIVE® Pinto or Kidney Beans

6 cups cold water

1¾ teaspoons THRIVE® Iodized Salt, divided

1 cup THRIVE® Cooked Ground Beef *(FD)*
or THRIVE® Beef TVP

1 tablespoon THRIVE® Chopped Onions *(FD)*

1 tablespoon THRIVE® Mixed Bell Peppers

1 cup THRIVE® Sweet Corn *(FD)*

1 (14.5 oz) can diced tomatoes, undrained

2 teaspoons chili powder

½ cup THRIVE® Shredded Cheddar
Cheese, rehydrated

1 tablespoon flour + 2 teaspoons water

1 Place washed and drained beans, cold water, and 1 teaspoon salt in a large saucepan. Bring to boil, then cover and simmer for 1 hour and 30 minutes.

2 While beans cook, place beef or TVP in a small bowl and cover with warm water. Let sit for 5-10 minutes until softened or rehydrated. Drain.

3 Add rehydrated ground beef, onions, bell peppers, corn, tomatoes, chili powder, and remaining ¾ teaspoon salt to beans. Simmer an additional 20 minutes.

4 Combine 1 tablespoon flour with 2 tablespoons water; stir into stew. Cook and stir until thick and bubbly. Stir in cheese and serve with any desired garnishes and toppings.

Main Dishes

84

RASPBERRY PORK CHOPS

Fix this savory and sweet meal for dinner and your guests will think you attended a premier culinary arts academy.

SERVES 4 • PREP TIME: 15 min • TOTAL TIME: 25 min

4 pork chops
½ teaspoon dried sage
½ teaspoon dried thyme
½ teaspoon THRIVE® Iodized Salt
½ cup THRIVE® Orange Drink
  (1½ teaspoons powder + ½ cup water)
½ cup orange juice
½ cup THRIVE® Raspberries *(FD)*
2 tablespoons red wine vinegar
  olive oil

1 Place raspberries in a bowl and cover with juice and orange drink. Set aside allowing raspberries to rehydrate. Season chops with salt and herbs on both sides.

2 Preheat a frying pan and drizzle with olive oil. Place chops in the pan. Sear on both sides, cooking through. Remove chops from pan.

3 Deglaze pan with juice, berries, and vinegar. Allow the raspberry sauce to continue cooking and reducing over medium heat until thickened and syrupy.

4 Serve sauce over chops. Sauce also goes nicely with chicken.

THRIVE® FOODS

Raspberries
Orange Drink
Iodized Salt

RICH & CREAMY CAULIFLOWER BAKE

This recipe is loaded with healthy veggies and flavorful cheese. The veggies are baked so perfectly that even your kids will ask for seconds.

SERVES 6 • PREP TIME: 30 min • TOTAL TIME: 50 min

1 tablespoon butter
1 tablespoon THRIVE® White Flour or Whole Wheat Flour
1 cup THRIVE® Powdered Milk, rehydrated
   (3 tablespoons powder + 1 cup water)
2 tablespoons heavy cream
½ teaspoon nutmeg
½ teaspoon THRIVE® Iodized Salt
1 cup THRIVE® Shredded Mozzarella Cheese, divided
1½ cups THRIVE® Broccoli *(FD)*
1½ cups THRIVE® Cauliflower *(FD)*
3 tablespoons Parmesan cheese, grated

1 In a medium-sized bowl, cover broccoli and cauliflower with warm water. Let sit 5-10 minutes until softened and rehydrated. Drain. Repeat same process for cheese.

2 Preheat oven to 350°F.

3 Meanwhile, melt butter in a medium-sized saucepan. Whisk in flour and cook for one minute. Next, whisk in prepared milk, stirring quickly to avoid lumps. Continue stirring over heat for about 2-3 minutes while sauce thickens.

4 Add cream, nutmeg, salt, and ⅔ cup of mozzarella cheese. Stir to combine and remove from heat.

5 Add well-drained broccoli and cauliflower. Gently stir together, adding salt and pepper to taste.

6 Place mixture in a greased 8 x 8 inch baking dish or a small pie plate. Top with remaining mozzarella and the Parmesan cheese. Bake for about 20 minutes or until hot, bubbly, and golden brown.

SIDE DISHES

The kitchen is a country in which there are always discoveries to be made.

Grimod de la Reynière

Confetti Rice, page 97

BLACK BEAN & RICE SALAD

This is my favorite side dish in the book. The beans paired with the rice and vegetables are so hearty and delicious. The tangy dressing provides the perfect balance of flavor.

SERVES 8 • PREP TIME: 15 min • TOTAL TIME: 1 hour 30 minutes

3 cups THRIVE® chicken broth
(3 teaspoons THRIVE® Chicken Bouillon + 3 cups water)

1½ cups THRIVE® White Rice

1½ cups THRIVE® Black Beans, rinsed and cooked

¼ cup THRIVE® Carrot Dices

¼ cup THRIVE® Mixed Bell Peppers

¼ cup THRIVE® Sweet Corn *(FD)*

½ red onion, diced

¼ cup red wine vinegar

1½ teaspoons Dijon mustard

3 tablespoons vegetable oil

THRIVE® Iodized Salt and pepper to taste

1 Cook beans for 1 to 1½ hours. For more information see page 13.

2 In a medium-sized bowl add carrot dices, mixed peppers, and sweet corn. Cover with warm water and let sit for 5-10 minutes until softened and rehydrated. Drain.

3 Place the chicken broth in a medium-sized saucepan. Bring to a boil over high heat. Add the rice and stir once. Cover, reduce heat to medium-low, and simmer for 20 minutes. Turn off heat and keep covered. Let rest for 5 minutes. Remove cover and fluff with a fork.

4 In a large bowl, combine cooked rice, cooked black beans, carrots, mixed bell peppers, corn, and red onion.

5 In a separate small bowl, whisk the vinegar, mustard, and oil until combined. Season with salt and pepper to taste. Toss rice mixture with dressing and serve.

SUMMER POTATO SALAD

A great side dish for the summer months.
Chill it in the fridge and take it to a bbq.

SERVES 4 • PREP TIME: 15 min • TOTAL TIME: 20 min

1½ cups THRIVE® Potato Dices *(FD)*
½ cup THRIVE® Diced Ham *(FD)*
½ cup THRIVE® Celery *(FD)*
½ cup THRIVE® Chopped Onions *(FD)*
½ cup mayonnaise
1½ teaspoons Dijon mustard
    THRIVE® Iodized Salt and pepper to taste
    green onions, chopped, *optional*

1 In a medium-sized bowl add potato dices, ham, celery, and onion and cover with water. Let sit for 5-10 minutes or until ingredients are rehydrated and soft. Drain.

2 In a large mixing bowl add all ingredients with mayonnaise and Dijon mustard. Stir until combined. Season generously with salt and pepper to taste. Garnish with chopped green onions, if desired.

3 Chill for at least 1 hour before serving.

SIMPLE SPANISH RICE

This is the perfect side dish for a
weekday evening.

SERVES 8 • PREP TIME: 15 min • TOTAL TIME: 30 min

1 cup water
¼ cup THRIVE® Chopped Onions *(FD)*
¾ cup THRIVE® Mixed Bell Peppers
¾ cup THRIVE® Sweet Corn *(FD)*
1½ cups salsa
2 cups THRIVE® chicken broth *(2 teaspoons THRIVE® Chicken Bouillon + 2 cups water)*
1½ cups THRIVE® White Rice
    THRIVE® Iodized Salt to taste

1 In a large skillet, add water, onions, mixed bell peppers and bring to a boil. Cook for about 10 minutes until onions and peppers are rehydrated and soft, water should be boiled off.

2 Add corn, salsa, and broth to skillet and bring to a boil. Stir in rice and cover. Simmer for 15 minutes, stirring occasionally. Remove from heat and let stand for 10 minutes.

3 Fluff with a fork before serving.

SOUR CREAM & CHEESE POTATOES

These potatoes will please all your guests.

SERVES 4 • PREP TIME: 20 min • TOTAL TIME: 45 min

4 cups THRIVE® Potato Chunks

1 can cream of chicken soup

2 cups THRIVE® Sour Cream
(2 cups powder + 1 cup water)

1 cup THRIVE® Chopped Onions *(FD)*

2 cups THRIVE® Shredded Cheddar Cheese *(FD)*

2 tablespoons butter
THRIVE® Iodized Salt and pepper to taste

1 Preheat oven to 350°F. In a large bowl, cover potato chunks with hot or boiling water. Let sit for 15 minutes. Drain. Repeat process for freeze-dried onions and cheese if necessary, allowing to sit for 5-10 minutes before draining.

2 Spread potatoes in the bottom of a casserole dish and set aside. In a medium-sized saucepan, combine soup, prepared sour cream, onions, butter, and 1½ cups of cheese. Heat the mixture over medium heat, stirring frequently, until the cheese is melted.

3 Pour cheese blend over the potatoes and combine; season with salt and pepper to taste. Top with remaining cheese and bake until the cheese is melted.

GARLIC MASHED POTATOES

Whether it's Thanksgiving or any other Thursday, mashed potatoes always hit the spot.

SERVES 8 • PREP TIME: 15 min • TOTAL TIME: 15 min

- 4 cups water
- 1½ teaspoons THRIVE® Iodized Salt
- 6 tablespoons butter
- 1⅓ cups THRIVE® Powdered Milk
  (4 tablespoons powder + 1⅓ cups water)
- 4 cups THRIVE® Potato Beads
- ¼ cup vegetable oil
- ¼ cup THRIVE® Sour Cream Powder, dry
- 1 can evaporated milk *(9 tablespoons THRIVE® Powdered Milk + 1½ cups water)*
- 1 teaspoon garlic powder
  THRIVE® Iodized Salt and pepper to taste

1 In a large saucepan, add water, salt, and butter and bring to a boil. Add prepared milk and potato beads. Stir to moisten and set aside.

2 In a medium-sized bowl, combine remaining ingredients. Stir in potatoes until well blended. Season with salt and pepper to taste.

CLASSIC GRAVY

What are potatoes without the savory flavor of gravy?

SERVES 4-6 • PREP TIME: 20 min • TOTAL TIME: 45 min

- 4 tablespoons butter
- 1 cup THRIVE® Powdered Milk, dry
- ¼ cup THRIVE® White Flour
- 3 cups water
- 3 teaspoons THRIVE® Chicken Bouillon
- ¾ teaspoon THRIVE® Iodized Salt
- ¾ teaspoon pepper

1 In a medium-sized saucepan, melt butter. Whisk in powdered milk and flour. Gradually add the water and whisk in the chicken bouillon. Add salt and pepper and cook over medium heat, stirring constantly until gravy is thickened and smooth. Remove from heat.

Tip *from the* **Kitchen**

If available, you can substitute any pan drippings for butter in this recipe.

HAM FRIED RICE

This rice brings the delicious tastes of Asia right to your table.

SERVES 4 • PREP TIME: 15 min • TOTAL TIME: 30 min

3½ cups THRIVE® chicken broth
   (3½ teaspoons THRIVE® Chicken Bouillon + 3½ cups water)

1¾ cup THRIVE® Instant White Rice

¼ cup THRIVE® Carrot Dices

½ cup THRIVE® Green Peas *(FD)*

¼ cup THRIVE® Chopped Onions *(FD)*

½ cup THRIVE® Diced Ham *(FD)* or THRIVE® Ham TVP

2 THRIVE® Whole Eggs, rehydrated
   (2 tablespoons powder + ¼ cup water)

1 tablespoon vegetable oil

1 teaspoon THRIVE® Iodized Salt

6 tablespoons soy sauce

½ teaspoon sesame or vegetable oil, *optional*

1 Boil 3½ cups water and chicken bouillon with instant white rice. Reduce to a simmer and cover for 5-10 minutes or until broth is absorbed. Remove from heat and let stand for 5 minutes. Set aside.

2 In a saucepan, add carrot dices, green peas, chopped onions, and ham with 4 cups of water and bring to a boil. Reduce to a simmer for 10 minutes or until vegetables and meat are tender. Drain and set aside.

3 Mix whole egg powder with ¼ cup water and pour into a greased frying pan. Cook as scrambled eggs. Set aside.

4 Heat a frying pan or wok over medium-high heat. Add 1 tablespoon vegetable oil and swirl to coat. Add rice and vegetable mixture to wok and stir fry 2 minutes until heated through. Add salt, soy sauce, and sesame oil. Gently add eggs into the rice mixture. Serve warm.

THRIVE

RICE PILAF

Use this recipe to add some flair and style to simple white rice.

SERVES 6 • PREP TIME: 25 min • TOTAL TIME: 1 hour 30 min

- 5 tablespoons butter
- 2 cups THRIVE® White Rice
- 4 cups THRIVE® chicken broth
  (4 teaspoons THRIVE® Chicken Bouillon + 4 cups water)
- ¾ cup THRIVE® Celery *(FD)*
- ¾ cup THRIVE® Carrot Dices
- ¾ cup THRIVE® Chopped Onions *(FD)*
- ⅔ cup almonds, slivered
  THRIVE® Iodized Salt and pepper to taste

1 Preheat oven to 375°F. In a small saucepan, bring chicken broth to a boil.

2 Melt butter in a large skillet. Brown rice lightly in butter. Place in casserole dish with boiling chicken broth. Cover and bake for 30 minutes.

3 Remove rice from oven and add vegetables and nuts, stirring and mixing well with a fork. Cover and return to oven for an additional 15 minutes.

4 Remove from oven and fluff with fork before serving.

THRIVE® FOODS

White Rice
♻ Celery
♻ Carrot Dices
♻ Chopped Onions
Iodized Salt

♻ - May be exchanged for fresh ingredients.

CONFETTI RICE

This recipe tastes as good as it looks.

SERVES 4 • PREP TIME: 5 min • TOTAL TIME: 30 min

- 1 tablespoon vegetable oil
- 1 small onion, diced *or 1 cup THRIVE® Chopped Onions (FD) + 1 cup water*
- 1 clove garlic, minced
- 2½ cups THRIVE® chicken broth *(2½ teaspoons THRIVE® Chicken Bouillon + 2½ cups water)*
- ¾ cup THRIVE® White Rice
- ¼ cup THRIVE® Mixed Bell Peppers *(FD)*
- ¼ cup THRIVE® Green Peas *(FD)*
- ¼ cup THRIVE® Sweet Corn *(FD)*
- ¾ teaspoon ground turmeric
- 1 teaspoon THRIVE® Iodized Salt

1 In a large saucepan or skillet, heat oil over medium heat. Add onion and garlic; cook, stirring constantly until onion is tender. Add chicken broth, rice, bell peppers, peas, corn, turmeric and salt. Cover and simmer for about 15 minutes.

2 Remove from heat. Cover and let stand for about 10 minutes or until heated through and liquid is absorbed.

CHEESE BLEND VEGGIE SAUCE

Give your vegetables an extra boost of flavor with this creamy cheese sauce.

SERVES 4 • PREP TIME: 15 min • TOTAL TIME: 15 min

- 1½ cups THRIVE® Instant Milk *(9 tablespoons powder + 1½ cups water)*
- ½ cup THRIVE® Cheese Blend powder
  Your choice of steamed vegetables

1 Combine milk with cheese blend in sauce pan over medium heat. Continue cooking while stirring for 10 minutes or until sauce reaches desired consistency.

2 Serve over steamed vegetables or as a dipping sauce.

Side Dishes

BOSTON BAKED BEANS

Don't forget the beans at your next barbecue! They take little effort and deliver big on flavor.

SERVES 8 • PREP TIME: 10 min • TOTAL TIME: 5 hours 10 min

  2 cups THRIVE® Small White Navy Beans
½ cup THRIVE® Bacon TVP
¼ cup THRIVE® Chopped Onions
½ cup molasses
¼ cup THRIVE® Brown Sugar
  1 teaspoon THRIVE® Iodized Salt
  2 teaspoons dry mustard
  2 teaspoons Worcestershire sauce

1 Sort the navy beans removing all broken beans. Soak beans (preferably overnight). Rinse beans before placing in slow cooker. Cover completely with new water. Cook on high for 4-5 hours or until beans are tender. Drain beans; reserving liquid.

2 Add bacon, 1 cup reserved bean liquid, chopped onion, molasses, brown sugar, salt, mustard, and Worcestershire sauce to slow cooker. Continue cooking on high, stirring occasionally, for at least 1 hour until the consistency of the sauce is to your liking. Season to taste.

THRIVE® FOODS

- ♻ Chopped Onions
- Navy Beans
- ♻ Bacon TVP
- Brown Sugar
- Iodized Salt

♻ - May be exchanged for fresh ingredients.

TACO SALAD

This salad is perfect for serving large groups because toppings can be altered to please even the pickiest of eaters.

SERVES 4 • PREP TIME: 15 min • TOTAL TIME: 15 min

1 cup THRIVE® Taco TVP
¼ cup THRIVE® Mixed Bell Peppers
½ cup THRIVE® Chopped Onions *(FD)*
2 cloves garlic, minced
2 tablespoons cilantro, minced
lettuce
tomatoes, *optional*
THRIVE® Shredded Cheddar Cheese, *optional*
THRIVE® Sour Cream, *optional*

1 In a medium-sized bowl, cover TVP with warm water. Let sit 5-10 minutes until softened and rehydrated. Drain. Repeat process for bell peppers and onions.

2 Brown meat or warm TVP in a frying pan. Combine with other ingredients. Serve over lettuce, tortillas, or corn chips with desired toppings and garnishes.

WHEAT BERRY SALAD
A great way to use your Thrive® Hard White Winter Wheat.

SERVES 4 • PREP TIME: 10 min • TOTAL TIME: 1 hour 30 min

- 2 cups THRIVE® Hard White Winter Wheat berries
  (see preparation instructions below)
- 1 cup THRIVE® freeze-dried berries *(any variety)*
- ½ cup walnuts or pecans
- ¼ cup THRIVE® drink (Apple, Orange or Peach), prepared
- ¼ cup raspberry vinaigrette dressing

For wheat berries:
1 Wash two cups of hard white winter wheat. Put wheat together with 7 cups cold water in a large pot. Bring to a boil, stir, and turn heat down to simmer.

2 Simmer wheat for one hour, stirring every ten minutes. Drain excess water from wheat. Wheat berries can be used immediately or stored in the refrigerator for later use.

For salad:
1 In a small bowl, cover berries with warm water and let sit 5-10 minutes or until softened and rehydrated. Drain.

2 Mix berries and cooked wheat berries in a medium-sized bowl. Toss in nuts, prepared drink mix, and raspberry vinaigrette. Stir to combine. Let stand for 1 hour. Spoon mixture onto a plate and serve at room temperature. Salad can also be chilled.

DESSERTS

All I really need is love, but a little chocolate now and then doesn't hurt!

Charles M. Schulz

Marbled Strawberry Cheesecake, page 119

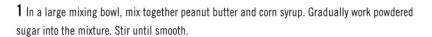

PEANUT BUTTER CHEWS

Peanut butter and chocolate treats—what could be better?

SERVES 12 • PREP TIME: 10 min • TOTAL TIME: 10 min

½ cup peanut butter
½ cup corn syrup
1 cup THRIVE® Powdered Sugar
⅓ cup THRIVE® Powdered Milk, dry
½ cup semi-sweet chocolate, melted

1 In a large mixing bowl, mix together peanut butter and corn syrup. Gradually work powdered sugar into the mixture. Stir until smooth.

2 Slowly add dry milk and mix until mixture is stiff enough to handle. Roll into shapes about ½ inch by 1 inch long and dip into melted chocolate. Allow chews to chill before serving.

Tip *from the* Kitchen

Add ⅛ cup more THRIVE® Powdered Milk for a firmer candy.

CHOCOLATE CAKE

This chocolate cake, made entirely from scratch, is sure to satisfy even your biggest chocolate cravings.

SERVES 6 • PREP TIME: 20 min • TOTAL TIME: 1 hour

1⅔ cups THRIVE® White Flour
1 cup THRIVE® Brown Sugar, packed
¼ cup unsweetened cocoa powder
1 teaspoon THRIVE® Baking Soda
½ teaspoon THRIVE® Iodized Salt
1 cup water
⅓ cup vegetable oil
1 teaspoon white vinegar
½ teaspoon vanilla

1 Preheat oven to 350°F. In a large mixing bowl, mix dry ingredients: flour, brown sugar, cocoa powder, baking soda, and salt. In another mixing bowl, add wet ingredients: water, oil, vinegar, and vanilla. Mix just until combined.

2 Pour batter into an ungreased 9 inch cake pan. Bake for 35-40 minutes, or until a toothpick inserted in the center comes out clean.

3 Remove cake from oven and let cool. Dust with powdered sugar or frost with icing just before serving.

THRIVE® FOODS

White Flour
Brown Sugar
Baking Soda
Iodized Salt

THRIVE® FOODS

Whole Wheat Flour
Quick Oats
↻ Powdered Milk
↻ Whole Eggs
White Sugar
Brown Sugar
Baking Soda
Iodized Salt

↻ - May be exchanged for fresh ingredients.

OATMEAL CAKE

If you are looking for a delicious and distinctive cake, look no further. This moist cake has a light oatmeal and coconut flavor that is always a crowd pleaser.

SERVES 12 • PREP TIME: 25 min • TOTAL TIME: 1 hour

1¼ cups boiling water
½ cup butter, softened and divided
1 cup THRIVE® Quick Oats
1 cup THRIVE® Brown Sugar
1½ cups THRIVE® White Sugar, divided
2 THRIVE® Whole Eggs, rehydrated
   (2 tablespoons powder + ¼ cup water)
1⅓ cups THRIVE® Whole Wheat Flour
1 teaspoon THRIVE® Baking Soda
1 teaspoon cinnamon
½ teaspoon nutmeg
½ teaspoon THRIVE® Iodized Salt
1 cup chopped nuts, *optional*
1 cup coconut
1 teaspoon vanilla
¼ cup THRIVE® Powdered Milk, rehydrated
   (¾ tablespoon powder + ¼ cup water)

For Frosting:
½ cup THRIVE® Powdered Milk, rehydrated
   (1¾ tablespoons powder + ½ cup water)
1 cup THRIVE® Brown Sugar
6 tablespoons butter, melted
1 teaspoon vanilla
1 cup coconut

1 Preheat oven to 350°F.

2 Mix boiling water, ¼ cup butter, and quick oats together; set aside.

3 In a separate bowl, mix brown sugar, 1 cup white sugar, and eggs. Add oatmeal mixture to creamed mixture; mix to combine.

4 Add whole wheat flour, baking soda, cinnamon, nutmeg, and salt. Mix thoroughly. Place in a greased 9 x 13 inch pan. Bake for 35 minutes.

5 While cake is baking, combine the rest of the ingredients (chopped nuts, coconut, remaining sugar, vanilla, remaining butter, and milk) and mix well.

6 Spread the topping mixture over the baked cake. Turn oven to broil and place cake back in the oven for 2-5 minutes, allowing the top of the cake to turn a light brown.

For Frosting:

1 In a saucepan over low heat, stir milk and sugar until dissolved. Add melted butter and stir, followed by the vanilla and coconut. Stir together until combined.

2 Pour frosting mixture over cake while it's still hot and fresh from the oven. Serve warm.

↻ - May be exchanged for fresh ingredients.

CHOCOLATE RASPBERRY SHORTCAKES

This recipe makes my mouth water just looking at the title! The rich chocolate shortcakes are delicious and the raspberry filing is the perfect flavor combination.

SERVES 4 • PREP TIME: 30 min • TOTAL TIME: 45 min

shortcakes:
- ¼ cup unsweetened cocoa powder
- 1 cup THRIVE® White Flour
- ¼ cup THRIVE® White Sugar
- 1½ teaspoons THRIVE® Baking Powder
- ½ teaspoon THRIVE® Baking Soda
- ¼ teaspoon THRIVE® Iodized Salt
- 4 tablespoons cold unsalted butter, cubed
- ½ cup heavy cream

raspberry filling:
- 3 cups THRIVE® Raspberries *(FD)*
- 2 tablespoons THRIVE® White Sugar, or to taste
- 2 teaspoons vanilla extract
  Vanilla Whipped Topping, see page 127.

1 Preheat oven to 425°F.

2 Make the shortcakes: In a large mixing bowl, sift together the cocoa powder, flour, sugar, baking powder, baking soda, and salt. Cut in the cold butter with a fork or pastry cutter. Blend the mixture until it resembles coarse meal. Add the heavy cream and stir the mixture with a fork until it forms a dough.

3 Roll out dough on a floured surface (dough should be ¼ inch thick). Using a biscuit cutter or top of a drinking glass, cut out 4 shortcakes. Place shortcakes on a lightly greased baking sheet, and bake the shortcakes for 12 minutes, or until a tester inserted in the centers comes out clean. Transfer the shortcakes to a wire rack and let them cool.

4 In a small bowl, cover the raspberries with warm water. Let sit for 5-10 minutes until softened and rehydrated. Drain. In another bowl mash ¾ cup of the rehydrated raspberries with a fork stirring in the white sugar and vanilla. Incorporate the remaining raspberries.

5 Carefully cut the shortcakes in half horizontally with a serrated knife. With a metal spatula transfer the bottom half of each to an individual plate. Top each bottom half with a spoonful of raspberry sauce and a dollop of vanilla whipped topping. Top the shortcakes with the top half and dust with powdered sugar, if desired.

Desserts

DOUBLE CHOCOLATE CHIP COOKIES

Double the chocolate is sure to double the smiles.

SERVES 18 • PREP TIME: 15 min • TOTAL TIME: 25 min

1 cup butter, softened
1 cup THRIVE® White Sugar
¾ cup THRIVE® Brown Sugar, packed
2 THRIVE® Whole Eggs, rehydrated
  (2 tablespoons powder + ¼ cup water)
¼ teaspoon THRIVE® Iodized Salt
2 teaspoons vanilla
1¾ cups THRIVE® White Flour
1¼ cups cocoa powder
2 teaspoons THRIVE® Baking Soda
1½ cups chocolate chips

1 Preheat oven to 350°F and grease cookie sheet or line with parchment paper.

2 In a large bowl, cream together the butter, white sugar, and brown sugar until light and fluffy. Add eggs, salt, and vanilla.

3 In another bowl, combine the flour, cocoa, and baking soda; gradually add to the creamed mixture. Mix well.

4 Stir in chocolate chips. Drop dough by spoonfuls onto the greased cookie sheet.

5 Bake for 8-10 minutes until cookies are fluffy, but still soft. Allow cookies to cool on baking sheet for 5 minutes before removing to a wire rack to cool completely.

CHOCOLATE CHIP COOKIES

Classic chocolate chip cookies always bring warmth and happiness to your loved ones.

SERVES 24 • PREP TIME: 15 min • TOTAL TIME: 30 min

1 cup butter, softened
1 cup THRIVE® White Sugar
1 cup THRIVE® Brown Sugar, packed
3 THRIVE® Whole Eggs, rehydrated
  (3 tablespoons powder + 6 tablespoons water)
2 teaspoons vanilla extract
1 teaspoon THRIVE® Baking Soda
¾ teaspoon THRIVE® Iodized Salt
2½ cups THRIVE® White Flour
2 cups chocolate chips or chunks

1 Preheat oven to 350°F.

2 In a large mixing bowl, whip butter. Add white sugar and brown sugar. Whip together for about 5 minutes.

3 Slowly add prepared eggs, while constantly stirring the mixture. Add vanilla, baking soda, and salt. Blend well.

4 Sift in flour and gently stir to incorporate. Increase speed and blend for another 5 minutes. Mix in chocolate chips.

5 Using spoons, hands, or a cookie scoop, place cookie dough portions onto a greased cookie sheet or line with parchment paper.

6 Bake for 8-12 minutes or until cookies turn golden brown.

WHOLE WHEAT OATMEAL COOKIES

*The delicious oats and whole wheat in these cookies
add a healthy touch to dessert.*

SERVES 12 • PREP TIME: 20 min • TOTAL TIME: 30 min

½ cup butter, softened

1 cup THRIVE® White Sugar

1½ cups THRIVE® Whole Wheat Flour

1¼ cups THRIVE® Quick Oats

½ teaspoon THRIVE® Baking Soda

½ teaspoon THRIVE® Iodized Salt

½ teaspoon cinnamon

¼ teaspoon nutmeg

1 THRIVE® Whole Egg, rehydrated
  (1 tablespoon powder + 2 tablespoons water)

¼ cup THRIVE® Powdered Milk, rehydrated
  (¾ tablespoon powder + ¼ cup water)

½ cup raisins, *optional*

½ cup nuts, *optional*

1 Preheat oven to 350°F.

2 In a large mixing bowl, cream together butter and sugar until light and fluffy.

3 In a separate bowl, mix all remaining dry ingredients (whole wheat flour, quick oats, baking soda, salt, cinnamon, and nutmeg). Mix dry ingredients with the sugar/butter mixture until fully incorporated.

4 Mix in prepared eggs and prepared milk. Once mixed, stir in raisins and nuts.

5 Drop dough by the teaspoonful onto a well-greased cookie sheet. Bake cookies for 10-12 minutes or until golden brown. Cookies will be flat and chewy.

CORNMEAL COOKIES

This cornmeal cookie won't disappoint. My favorite way to make them is with dried cranberries.

SERVES 12 • PREP TIME: 15 min • TOTAL TIME: 30 min

¾ cup butter, softened

¾ cup THRIVE® White Sugar

1 THRIVE® Whole Egg, rehydrated
    (1 tablespoon powder + 2 tablespoons water)

1 teaspoon lemon extract

½ cup THRIVE® Cornmeal

1 teaspoon THRIVE® Baking Powder

¼ teaspoon THRIVE® Iodized Salt

1½ cups THRIVE® White Flour

½ cup dried cranberries or raisins

1 Preheat oven to 375°F.

2 In a large mixing bowl, cream together butter and sugar until light and fluffy. Mix in the egg and lemon extract. Mix well.

3 In a separate mixing bowl, combine the cornmeal, baking powder, salt, and flour.

4 Add the flour mixture to the butter mixture and combine. Stir in dried cranberries or raisins.

5 Drop batter by teaspoonfuls onto a lightly greased baking sheet. Bake for 10-12 minutes, until the cookie bottoms are lightly browned.

6 Let cookies cool for 2 minutes on baking sheet before placing them on a cooling rack.

ALMOND APRICOT THUMBPRINT COOKIES

You can make this recipe with any of the Thrive® fruits. I've made them with raspberries and blackberries and they are always delicious.

SERVES 12 (2 dozen cookies) • PREP TIME: 15 min • TOTAL TIME: 30 min

¾ cup butter, softened
½ cup THRIVE® White Sugar
1 THRIVE® Whole Egg, rehydrated
  (1 tablespoon powder + 2 tablespoons water)
½ teaspoon almond extract
1¾ cups THRIVE® White Flour
  THRIVE® Powdered Sugar, for dusting

For Apricot Preserves:
1 cup THRIVE® Apricots *(FD)*
¾ cup water
¼ cup THRIVE® White Sugar

Tip *from the* Kitchen

You may use store-bought apricot preserves, or puréed THRIVE® Apricots.

1 Preheat oven to 375°F.

2 Prepare Apricot Preserves. Bring freeze-dried apricots and water to a simmer in a saucepan over medium-high heat. Simmer for 5 minutes, stirring frequently. Add ¼ cup sugar and continue to simmer for another 5 minutes. Remove from heat and cool.

3 In a medium-sized bowl, cream together butter, sugar, prepared egg, and almond extract. Slowly mix in flour until a soft dough forms.

4 Roll dough into 1 inch balls. Place balls 2 inches apart onto ungreased baking sheets. Use your finger or an instrument of similar size to make a well in the center of each cookie. Fill the hole with ½ teaspoon of apricot preserves.

5 Bake for 8-10 minutes, until golden brown on the bottom. Remove from cookie sheets to cool on wire racks. Dust with powdered sugar, if desired.

Desserts

114

BLUEBERRY PEACH COBBLER

*Cobblers always remind me of summer nights. This
will be a crowd pleaser no matter when you serve it.*

SERVES 6 • PREP TIME: 20 min • TOTAL TIME: 1 hour

½ cup butter, softened
¾ cup THRIVE® White Sugar, divided
  zest of 1 lemon
2 THRIVE® Whole Eggs, rehydrated
  (2 tablespoons powder + ¼ cup water)
½ teaspoon vanilla extract
1 cup THRIVE® White Flour
1 teaspoon THRIVE® Baking Powder
½ teaspoon THRIVE® Iodized Salt
1 cup THRIVE® Peach Slices *(FD)*
1 cup THRIVE® Blueberries *(FD)*
1 cup THRIVE® Peach Drink, prepared
½ teaspoon cinnamon

1 In a medium-sized bowl, cover peach slices and blueberries with peach drink or warm water. Let sit 5-10 minutes until softened and rehydrated.

2 Preheat oven to 350°F.

3 In a medium-sized mixing bowl, mix together butter and ½ cup sugar. Add lemon zest, eggs, and vanilla extract.

4 In another bowl, sift together the flour, baking powder, and salt; add to the butter mixture, stirring to incorporate. Spread half of the batter on the bottom of a greased 8 x 8 x 2 inch baking dish.

5 Top the batter in the pan with the rehydrated peaches and blueberries, along with ½ of the hydrating liquid (about). Carefully spread the remaining batter over the top of the peaches. Sprinkle cinnamon and remaining sugar over the top.

6 Bake for 38-45 minutes, or until golden brown.
Serve hot with ice cream.

PEACH COBBLER CAKES
A little cake with a lot of flavor.

SERVES 24 • PREP TIME: 15 min • TOTAL TIME: 1 hour

3 cups THRIVE® White Flour
4 teaspoons THRIVE® Baking Powder
1 teaspoon THRIVE® Iodized Salt
1 cup THRIVE® White Sugar
1 cup THRIVE® Powdered Milk
   (6 tablespoons powder + 1 cup water)
½ cup butter, melted
1½ teaspoons vanilla extract
2 cups THRIVE® Peach Slices *(FD)*
¼ cup THRIVE® White Sugar, for sprinkling tops

1 In a small bowl, cover peaches with warm water or peach drink. Let sit 5-10 minutes until softened and rehydrated. Drain.

2 Preheat oven to 350°F. Generously grease muffin tin with non-stick cooking spray.

3 Combine all dry ingredients: flour, baking powder, salt, and sugar. Whisk in prepared milk followed by melted butter and vanilla.

4 Evenly distribute the rehydrated peaches at the bottom of each muffin slot. Pour ¼ cup batter on top of peaches. Sprinkle each muffin slot with remaining sugar.

5 Bake for 20-30 minutes or until golden brown. Cool cobbler cakes and flip out onto a cooling rack. Serve with vanilla ice cream or whipped topping.

APPLE CRISPS

This dessert is sugar, spice, and everything nice.

SERVES 4 • PREP TIME: 15 min • TOTAL TIME: 45 min

4 cups THRIVE® Apple Chips	
2-3 cups THRIVE® Apple Drink, prepared	
½ cup raisins	
¾ cup THRIVE® Brown Sugar	
½ cup THRIVE® White Flour	
½ cup THRIVE® Quick Oats	
½ teaspoon cinnamon	
½ teaspoon nutmeg	
8 tablespoons cold butter, cubed	

1 In a large bowl, cover apple chips and raisins with warm water or apple drink. Let sit 5-10 minutes until softened and rehydrated. Drain.

2 Preheat oven to 350°F.

3 Make a crumble by combining brown sugar, flour, oats, cinnamon, and nutmeg in a bowl. Cut in butter using a pastry cutter or fork until crumbly.

4 Divide apple mixture evenly between 4 individual, buttered ramekins or oven-proof baking dishes. Sprinkle crumble over the apple mixture in each dish.

5 Bake for 25 minutes or until apples are tender and topping is golden brown. Top each bowl with a scoop of ice cream or whipped topping.

MARBLED STRAWBERRY CHEESECAKE

This cheesecake boasts of the elegance and taste of a gourmet dessert, but the simplicity of the recipe will make you smile.

SERVES 8 • PREP TIME: 30 min • TOTAL TIME: 1 hour 30 min

- 3 cups THRIVE® Strawberries *(FD)*
- 1¼ cups THRIVE® White Sugar, divided
- 1½ teaspoons cornstarch
- ¼ cup butter, melted
- 1 cup graham cracker crumbs
- 24 oz cream cheese, softened
- 1 teaspoon vanilla
- 3 THRIVE® Whole Eggs, rehydrated
  (3 tablespoons powder + 6 tablespoons water)

1 In a small bowl, cover strawberries with warm water. Let sit 5-10 minutes until softened or rehydrated. Drain, reserving ¾ cup of water.

2 Combine strawberries, reserved water, 4 teaspoons of sugar, and cornstarch in a blender and purée. Heat puréed mixture in a small saucepan over medium heat until thickened (about 5-10 minutes). Allow mixture to cool in saucepan.

For Crust:

1 Preheat oven to 350°F. In a large mixing bowl, combine melted butter, graham cracker crumbs, and 3 tablespoons sugar for crust.

2 Press mixture onto bottom of 9 inch spring form pan. Bake for 10 minutes. Remove from the oven and cool.

For Cheesecake:

1 Preheat oven to 300°F. Using an electric mixer on medium speed, combine cream cheese, remaining sugar, and vanilla until well blended. Add prepared eggs to cream cheese blend, mixing well.

2 Cover graham cracker crust with ½ cheesecake batter. Take half of the strawberry mixture and add it to the remaining batter. Pour strawberry cheesecake batter mixture into the same pan, followed by the remaining strawberry mixture. Swirl the batter with a knife until it takes on a marbled effect.

3 Bake cheesecake for 60-70 minutes or until set. Remove cheesecake from the oven, allow it to cool, then remove cake from pan. Chill overnight before serving.

Desserts

119

BROWNIE LOLLIES

This recipe is a lot of fun. The more chocolate you add, the better it gets!

SERVES 12 • PREP TIME: 30 min • TOTAL TIME: 1 hour

2½ cups THRIVE® Fudge Brownie mix
6 tablespoons hot water

Chocolate Buttercream Frosting:
¼ tablespoon butter, softened
2 tablespoons THRIVE® Instant Milk
   (¾ tablespoon powder + 2 tablespoons water)
¼ cup melted chocolate
⅓ cup cocoa powder
2 cups THRIVE® Powdered Sugar
1 pinch THRIVE® Iodized Salt
   wooden popsicle sticks or sucker sticks
   additional melting chocolate, any variety

1 Preheat oven to 350°F.

2 Mix hot water with brownie mix. Bake in an 8 x 8 inch non-stick baking dish for 18 to 22 minutes.

3 Prepare chocolate buttercream frosting:
In a large mixing bowl, mix butter, milk, and chocolate on high speed until fully incorporated. Sift cocoa powder and powdered sugar together and slowly add to reach desired frosting consistency, followed by salt. Mix well. *(If needed, add more milk to thin out, more powdered sugar to thicken, and more cocoa powder to increase the chocolate flavor.)*

4 Remove brownies from oven and cool. Top with prepared frosting. Chill in refrigerator for 10 minutes.

5 Take frosted brownies and use an ice cream scoop with a release handle to create little lollipop balls. The frosting will act like a glue, keeping it all together.

6 Place balled brownies on a baking sheet lined with wax paper or parchment. Poke a popsicle stick or other handle into each lollipop and freeze for 30 minutes.

7 Meanwhile, melt additional chocolate (any variety). Once lollies are set up, dip into melted chocolate. After that chocolate has had a chance to cool on the lollies, drizzle with more chocolate.

CHOCOLATE FUDGE

Use as a delicious and thoughtful homemade holiday gift.

SERVES 32 • PREP TIME: 15 min • TOTAL TIME: 30 min

1 cup THRIVE® Powdered Milk, dry
1 cup THRIVE® White Sugar
2 tablespoons butter
½ cup hot water
2 teaspoons vanilla
¾ teaspoon THRIVE® Iodized Salt
1 pound chocolate, chopped

1 Line bottom of an 8 x 8 inch baking pan with parchment paper or wax paper.

2 Begin by making sweetened condensed milk in blender. Combine powdered milk, sugar, butter, and hot water in blender or food processor and mix until combined.

3 Add prepared sweetened condensed milk to a glass or stainless steel bowl; set over a pan of barely simmering water. Add vanilla, salt, and chopped chocolate stirring occasionally, until smooth. Add any additional ingredients that you desire: nuts, citrus zest, crushed candies, or flavored extracts.

4 Pour into prepared baking pan and chill, uncovered, until firm, about 4 hours. Run a knife around edges of pan and invert fudge onto a work surface. Remove parchment and cut fudge into 1-inch squares. Serve chilled.

 Tip *from the* **Kitchen**

This recipe makes a great base for adding extras like nuts, crushed candies, or extract flavors.

Desserts

LEMON BLINTZES & STRAWBERRY PURÉE

This dessert will tantalize your taste buds and make you feel like you are strolling down the shores of the French Riviera.

SERVES 6 • PREP TIME: 20 min • TOTAL TIME: 20 min

1½ cups THRIVE® White Flour

2 cups THRIVE® Powdered Milk, rehydrated
   (6 tablespoons powder + 2 cups water)

3 THRIVE® Whole Eggs, rehydrated
   (3 tablespoons powder + 6 tablespoons water)

1 teaspoon vegetable oil

½ teaspoon THRIVE® Iodized Salt

1 teaspoon vanilla
   zest and juice from 1 lemon

1 tablespoon butter

1 cup THRIVE® Strawberries *(FD)*

½ cup THRIVE® Peach Drink, prepared

1 For the purée, combine strawberries, peach drink, sugar, and lemon juice in a food processor or blender. Let strawberries absorb moisture, then blend until smooth. Set aside and begin work on lemon blintzes.

2 Combine flour, milk, eggs, oil, salt, vanilla, and lemon zest; gently mix.

3 Heat skillet and grease with butter. Add a small amount of batter to the skillet; move pan in circular motions to get the batter to spread as thinly as possible.

4 Flip and cook the other side until browned. Fill with strawberry purée to taste, serve warm.

Tip from the **Kitchen**

The same crepe recipe may also be used with savory fillings like cheeses and meats.

TRIPLE BERRY PIE

What's more America then apple pie? Nothing, but this Triple Berry Pie is pretty delicious.

SERVES 8 • PREP TIME: 30 min • TOTAL TIME: 1 hour 10 min

Pie Crust:
- 2 cups THRIVE® White Flour
- 1 teaspoon THRIVE® Iodized Salt
- ⅔ cup shortening
- 4½ tablespoons cold water

Filling:
- 2 cups THRIVE® Blackberries *(FD)*
- 2 cups THRIVE® Blueberries *(FD)*
- 2 cups THRIVE® Raspberries *(FD)*
- 2 teaspoons lemon juice
- 1 cup THRIVE® White Sugar
- 3 tablespoons THRIVE® White Flour

1 Preheat oven to 450°F.

2 In a small bowl, cover berries in warm water. Lct sit 5-10 minutes or until softened and rehydrated. Drain.

3 Stir together berries and lemon juice. Set aside. Mix sugar and flour. Add to berry mixture. Set aside.

4 Sift together flour and salt. Using a pastry blender, cut in shortening until pieces are pea-size. Sprinkle water in 1 tablespoon at a time, until the dough is moistened. Divide in half. Form each half into a ball. Roll one ball into a 12-inch circle and transfer to pie dish.

5 Pour berry filling into the bottom crust.

6 Roll remaining dough into a circle. Place on filling. Crimp edges and cut slits to allow the steam to escape.

7 Bake for 10 minutes. Reduce heat to 350°F and cook for 30 minutes or until golden brown.

FRENCH VANILLA CREPES & WHITE CHOCOLATE STRAWBERRY MOUSSE

This gourmet French dessert will have you saying ooh la la!

SERVES 12 • PREP TIME: 30 min • TOTAL TIME: 45 min

1½ cups THRIVE® Powdered Milk, rehydrated
   (4½ tablespoons powder + 1½ cups water)

 3 THRIVE® Whole Eggs, rehydrated
   (3 tablespoons powder + 6 tablespoons water)

 2 tablespoons vanilla

1½ cups THRIVE® White Flour

 2 tablespoons THRIVE® White Sugar

 ½ teaspoon THRIVE® Iodized Salt

 5 tablespoons butter, melted

Mousse:

1½ cups THRIVE® Strawberries *(FD)*

 3 tablespoons THRIVE® White Sugar

1¾ cups heavy cream

 6 oz white chocolate, chopped

1 In a large bowl, mix together the prepared milk, eggs and vanilla. Stir in the flour, sugar, salt, and melted butter until well blended.

2 Heat a sauté pan or crepe pan over medium heat until hot. Coat with vegetable oil or cooking spray. Pour ¼ cup of batter into the pan and tip to spread the batter to the edges. When bubbles form on the top and the edges are dry, flip over and cook until lightly browned on the other side and edges are golden. Repeat with remaining batter.

To make mousse:

1 In a small bowl, cover strawberries in warm water. Let sit 5-10 minutes or until softened and rehydrated. Drain. In another mixing bowl, sweeten drained strawberries by adding sugar and stir until sugar dissolves. Process in blender or food processor until sauce runs smooth. Makes 1 cup of sauce.

2 In a heavy saucepan over low heat, warm ¼ cup of the heavy cream and the white chocolate, stirring constantly until chocolate melts. Let mixture cool until it is lukewarm. Stir in 2 tablespoons of strawberry sauce. Transfer to a large bowl.

3 In a medium-sized bowl, whip remaining 1½ cups cream to soft peaks. Fold into melted chocolate mixture, one-third at a time, until no streaks remain. Layer into crepes, and serve with the strawberry sauce.

Tip *from the* **Kitchen**

You can also fill crepes with your favorite fruit, cream, caramel, ice cream, or cheese to serve.

Desserts

125

TRIPLE BERRY CRISP

I've been making this recipe for years. I used to make it with fresh or frozen berries, but now I make it with my Thrive® berries! Top it with vanilla ice cream to really seal the deal.

SERVES 8-10 • PREP TIME: 15 min • TOTAL TIME: 30 min

1½ cups THRIVE® Blackberries *(FD)*
1½ cups THRIVE® Raspberries *(FD)*
1½ cups THRIVE® Blueberries *(FD)*
2 tablespoons THRIVE® White Sugar
1 cup THRIVE® White Flour
1 cup THRIVE® Quick Oats
¾ cup THRIVE® Brown Sugar, packed
½ teaspoon ground cinnamon
¼ teaspoon ground nutmeg
¾ cup cold butter, cubed

1 Preheat oven to 350°F.

2 In a large bowl, cover all berries with warm water. Let sit 5-10 minutes until softened and rehydrated. Drain. Once berries have completely drained, cover with 2 tablespoons sugar in mixing bowl.

3 In a separate large bowl, combine flour, oats, brown sugar, cinnamon, and nutmeg. Cut in butter until crumbly with a fork or pastry cutter. Press half of mixture in the bottom of a 8 x 8 x 2 inch pan. Cover with berries. Sprinkle remaining crumble mixture over the berries.

4 Bake in the preheated oven for 30 to 40 minutes, or until fruit is bubbly and topping is golden brown.

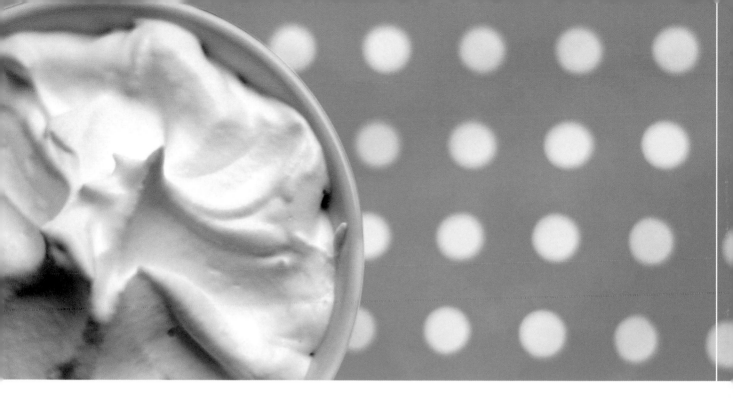

VANILLA WHIPPED TOPPING
Never buy frozen whipped topping again!

SERVES 4 (1 cup) • PREP TIME: 15 min • TOTAL TIME: 30 min

½ cup ice water
½ cup THRIVE® Instant Milk, dry
½ cup THRIVE® Powdered Sugar
1 teaspoon vanilla extract

1 Combine ice water and powdered milk in bowl, beat on high for 15-20 minutes. Add powered sugar and vanilla and continue to beat well until thoroughly blended. Chill. This works best in a stand mixer with whip beaters that have been chilled. If mixture begins to fall, beat again.

Note: You must use THRIVE® Instant Milk and not the standard dry milk variety.

GRAINS

VEGETABLES

Bell Peppers, Mixed
Bell Pepper Chicken, 82
Black Bean & Rice Salad, 90
Confetti Rice, 97
Green Chile Mexican Soup, 79
Pioneer Stew, 84
Quick & Easy Quesadillas, 18
Simple Spanish Rice, 91
Sweet & Sour Meatballs, 66
Taco Salad, 100
Taco Soup, 81
TVP Tacos, 69
Whole Wheat Meatloaf, 75

Broccoli
Rich & Creamy Cauliflower Bake, 86

Carrot Dices
Black Bean & Rice Salad, 90
Cauliflower Cheese Soup, 56
Chicken Pot Pie, 74
Chicken Vegetable Casserole, 76
Creamy Chicken Noodle Soup with Dumplings, 59
Ham Fried Rice, 94
Rice Pilaf, 96
Shepherd's Pie, 73

Cauliflower
Cauliflower Cheese Soup, 56
Rich & Creamy Cauliflower Bake, 86

Celery
Cauliflower Cheese Soup, 56
Chicken Pot Pie, 74
Chicken Salad Sandwich, 70
Chicken Vegetable Casserole, 76
Corn Chowder, 57
Creamy Chicken Noodle Soup with Dumplings, 59
Rice Pilaf, 96
Summer Potato Salad, 91

Green Peas
Chicken Pot Pie, 74
Confetti Rice, 97
Ham Fried Rice, 94
Shepherd's Pie, 73

Mushroom Pieces
Beef Stroganoff, 65

Onions, Chopped
Cauliflower Cheese Soup, 56
Chicken Salad Sandwich, 70
Chicken Vegetable Casserole, 76
Confetti Rice, 97
Corn Chowder, 57
Ham Fried Rice, 94
Pioneer Stew, 84
Rice Pilaf, 96
Simple Spanish Rice, 91
Sour Cream & Cheese Potatoes, 92
Summer Potato Salad, 91
Sweet & Sour Meatballs, 66
Taco Salad, 100
Taco Soup, 81
Whole Wheat Meatloaf, 75

Onions, Chopped (dehydrated)
Boston Baked Beans, 98
Creamy & Cheesy Potato Soup, 62
Mexican Tamale Pie, 63
Quick & Easy Quesadillas, 18
Refried Bean Burritos, 83

Shepherd's Pie, 73
Slow Cooked 3 Bean Chili, 60

Potato Beads
Garlic Mashed Potatoes, 93
Shepherd's Pie, 73

Potato Chunks
Sour Cream & Cheese Potatoes, 92

Potato Dices
Corn Chowder, 57
Creamy & Cheesy Potato Soup, 62
Summer Potato Salad, 91

Spinach, Chopped
Corn Chowder, 57

Sweet Corn
Beef Enchilada Bake, 68
Black Bean & Corn Salsa, 17
Black Bean & Rice Salad, 90
Chicken Vegetable Casserole, 76
Confetti Rice, 97
Corn Chowder, 57
Green Chile Mexican Soup, 79
Mexican Tamale Pie, 63
Pioneer Stew, 84
Simple Spanish Rice, 91

Sweet Potato
Sweet Potato Muffins, 31

Tomato Powder
Slow Cooked 3 Bean Chili, 60
Taco Soup, 81

FRUIT

Apple Chips
Apple Crisps, 117

Apple Slices
Apple Puff Pancakes, 40

Apricots
Almond Apricot Thumbprint Cookies, 114

Banana Slices
Banana Pancakes with Sweet Cream Cinnamon
Spread, 38

Strawberry Banana Freeze, 27

Blackberries
6 Grain Pancakes with Berry Compote, 37

Berry Smoothie, 27

Blackberry Muffin Cups, 30

Triple Berry Crisp, 126

Triple Berry Pie, 124

Very Orange Berry Smoothie, 27

Blueberries
6 Grain Pancakes with Berry Compote, 37

Blueberry Muffins with Streusel Topping, 32

Blueberry Peach Cobbler, 115

Chewy Granola Bars, 25

Coconut Almond Fruit Granola, 24

Triple Berry Crisp, 126

Triple Berry Pie, 124

Very Orange Berry Smoothie, 27

Peach Slices
Berry Smoothie, 27

Blueberry Peach Cobbler, 115

Peach Cobbler Cakes, 116

Peach Smoothie, 27

Pears
Coconut Almond Fruit Granola, 24

Pineapple Chunks
Strawberry Banana Freeze, 27

Raspberries
6 Grain Pancakes with Berry Compote, 37

Berry Cinnamon Rolls with Lemon Cream Cheese
Icing, 34

Chocolate Raspberry Shortcakes, 109

Coconut Almond Fruit Granola, 24

Germade with Berry Purée & Cream, 41

Raspberry Pork Chops, 85

Triple Berry Crisp, 126

Triple Berry Pie, 124

Very Orange Berry Smoothie, 27

Wheat Berry Salad, 101

Strawberries
Berry Cinnamon Rolls with Lemon Cream Cheese
Icing, 34

Chewy Granola Bars, 25

French Vanilla Crepes & White Chocolate Strawberry
Mousse, 125

Germade with Berry Purée & Cream, 41

Lemon Blintzes & Strawberry Purée, 122

Marbled Strawberry Cheesecake, 119

Strawberry Banana Freeze, 27

Very Orange Berry Smoothie, 27

Wheat Berry Salad, 101

DAIRY

Cheddar Cheese
Beef Enchilada Bake, 68

Cauliflower Cheese Soup, 56

Creamy & Cheesy Potato Soup, 62

Pioneer Stew, 84

Quick & Easy Quesadillas, 18

Refried Bean Burritos, 83

Shepherd's Pie, 73

Slow Cooked 3 Bean Chili, 60

Sour Cream & Cheese Potatoes, 92

Cheese Blend
Cheddar Cheese Crisps, 20

Cheese Blend Veggie Sauce, 97

Macaroni & Cheese, 71

Instant Milk
Beef Stroganoff, 65

Berry Smoothie, 27

Brownie Lollies, 120

Cheese Blend Veggie Sauce, 97

Chicken Pot Pie, 74

Creamy Chicken Noodle Soup with Dumplings, 59

Creamy & Cheesy Potato Soup, 62

Macaroni & Cheese, 71

Mexican Tamale Pie, 63

Pinto Bean Bread, 44

Whole Wheat Meatloaf, 75

Monterey Jack Cheese
Mexican Tamale Pie, 63

Mozzarella Cheese
Rich & Creamy Cauliflower Bake, 86

Powdered Milk
6 Grain Pancakes with Berry Compote, 37

Apple Puff Pancakes, 40

Banana Pancakes with Sweet Cream Cinnamon Spread, 38

Berry Cinnamon Rolls with Lemon Cream Cheese Icing, 34

Blueberry Muffins with Streusel Topping, 32

Chicken Vegetable Casserole, 76

Chocolate Fudge, 121

Classic Gravy, 93

Feather Rolls, 45

French Vanilla Crepes & White Chocolate Strawberry Mousse, 125

Garlic Mashed Potatoes, 93

Germade with Berry Purée & Cream, 41

Lemon Blintzes & Strawberry Purée, 122

Oatmeal Cake, 107

Peach Cobbler Cakes, 116

Peanut Butter Chews, 104

Rich & Creamy Cauliflower Bake, 86

Sweet & Sour Meatballs, 66

Sweet Potato Muffins, 31

Vanilla Whipped Topping, 127

Whole Wheat Crackers, 21

Whole Wheat Crepes, 41

Whole Wheat Oatmeal Cookies, 112

Sour Cream Powder
Beef Stroganoff, 65

Garlic Mashed Potatoes, 92

Refried Bean Burritos, 83

Slow Cooked 3 Bean Chili, 60

Sour Cream & Cheese Potatoes, 92

MEAT & BEANS

Bacon (TVP)
Boston Baked Beans, 98

Beans, Black
Black Bean & Corn Salsa, 17
Black Bean & Rice Burgers, 78
Black Bean & Rice Salad, 90
Slow Cooked 3 Bean Chili, 60

Beans, Kidney
Pioneer Stew, 84
Slow Cooked 3 Bean Chili, 60
Taco Soup, 81

Beans, Pinto
Black Bean & Corn Salsa, 17
Pinto Bean Bread, 44
Pioneer Stew, 84
Refried Bean Burritos, 83
Taco Soup, 81

Beans, White Navy Beans
Boston Baked Beans, 98
Green Chile Mexican Soup, 79
Slow Cooked 3 Bean Chili, 60

Beef (TVP)
Pioneer Stew, 84

Chicken Dices
Chicken Salad Sandwich, 70
Chicken Vegetable Casserole, 76
Creamy Chicken Noodle Soup with Dumplings, 59
Green Chile Mexican Soup, 79

Eggs
30 Minute Rolls, 45
6 Grain Pancakes with Berry Compote, 37
Almond Apricot Thumbprint Cookies, 114
Apple Puff Pancakes, 40
Bell Pepper Chicken, 82
Berry Cinnamon Rolls with Lemon Cream Cheese Icing, 34
Black Bean & Rice Burgers, 78
Blackberry Muffin Cups, 30
Blueberry Muffins with Streusel Topping, 32
Blueberry Peach Cobbler, 115
Chocolate Chip Cookies, 111
Cornmeal Cookies, 113
Double Chocolate Chips Cookies, 110
Feather Rolls, 45
French Vanilla Crepes & White Chocolate Strawberry Mousse, 125
Ham Fried Rice, 94
Homemade Cornbread, 42
Lemon Blintzes & Strawberry Purée, 122
Marbled Strawberry Cheesecake, 119
Mexican Tamale Pie, 63
Oatmeal Cake, 107
Sun-Dried Tomato Focaccia, 47
Sweet & Sour Meatballs, 66
Sweet Potato Muffins, 31
Whole Wheat Crepes, 41
Whole Wheat Meatloaf, 75
Whole Wheat Oatmeal Cookies, 112

Ground Beef
Beef Enchilada Bake, 68
Pioneer Stew, 84
Slow Cooked 3 Bean Chili, 60
Sweet & Sour Meatballs, 66
Whole Wheat Meatloaf, 75

Ham (TVP)
Ham Fried Rice, 94

Ham Dices
Ham Fried Rice, 94
Summer Potato Salad, 91

Roast Beef
Beef Stroganoff, 65
Shepherd's Pie, 73

Taco (TVP)
Mexican Tamale Pie, 68
Quick & Easy Quesadillas, 18
Taco Salad, 100
Taco Soup, 81
TVP Tacos, 69

BASICS

Apple Drink
6 Grain Pancakes with Berry Compote, 37
Germade with Berry Purée & Cream, 41
Sweet Potato Muffins, 31

Baking Powder
Found in various recipes

Baking Soda
Found in various recipes

Beef Bouillon
Shepherd's Pie, 73

Brown Sugar
Found in various recipes

Butter Powder
Macaroni & Cheese, 71

Chicken Bouillon
Black Bean & Rice Salad, 90
Cauliflower Cheese Soup, 56
Chicken Pot Pie, 74
Confetti Rice, 97
Creamy Potato Soup, 62
Green Chile Mexican Soup, 79
Ham Fried Rice, 94
Rice Pilaf, 96
Simple Spanish Rice, 91
Slow Cooked 3 Bean Chili, 60

Iodized Salt
Found in various recipes

Orange Drink
Raspberry Pork Chops, 85
Strawberry Banana Freeze, 27
Very Orange Berry Smoothie, 27

Peach Drink
6 Grain Pancakes with Berry Compote, 37
Berry Smoothie, 27
Blueberry Peach Cobbler, 115
Lemon Blitzes & Strawberry Purée, 122

Powdered Sugar
Apricot Thumbprint Cookies, 114
Peanut Butter Chews, 104

White Sugar
Found in various recipes